THE BEST

AMAZING TRUE

MISSION STORIES

FROM AROUND THE WORLD

J. H. ZACHARY

Pacific Press® Publishing Association
Nampa, Idaho
Oshawa, Ontario, Canada
www.pacificpress.com

Cover Design by Michelle C. Petz
Cover art (globe) Getty Images

Copyright © 2003 by
Pacific Press® Publishing Association
Printed in the United States of America
All Rights Reserved

Additional copies of this book may be purchased online at
www.adventistbookcenter.com

Library of Congress Cataloging-in-Publication Data

Zachary, J. H., 1929-
Amazing true mission stories : the best from around the world / J. H. Zachary.
p. cm.
ISBN: 0-8163-1982-0
1. Missionary stories. I. Title.

BV2087.Z33 2003
266'.6732—dc21   2003040558

03 04 05 06 07 • 5 4 3 2 1

DEDICATION

To my parents, Viva and Jack Zachary,
whose prayers and guidance have made it possible for me to become
what I am today. Although ninety-eight years old,
my mother still prays daily for me and my wife
as we travel around the world. To better understand
the environment in which I grew up, you may enjoy
reading my dad's story, *Into the Blizzard*,
which has recently been reprinted.

ACKNOWLEDGMENTS

The publication of this book is the result of many helping hands. I appreciate the permission of Charlotte Iskhanian to include several stories that appeared first in *Inside Story*. The encouragement and support of Dr. Gayle Wilson, who has presented health lectures for my evangelism programs in several countries, opened the door for the publication of this book to become a reality.

Jeane, my life partner of fifty-three years, spent many hours typing, editing, and taking notes on site during several mission trips. During fifty-one years in ministry, she has been a missionary widow for about twenty years as a result of the many trips that have separated us. I greatly appreciate her love and support.

Pastor Paterno Diaz, retired president of the South Philippine Union Conference, gave counsel and support for many of the stories from the Philippines. Dr. Fred Webb graciously shared with me many of the stories from Mountain View College in the Philippines, where he organized and directed outreach activities for several years.

Mrs. Dorothy Watts also kindly gave us permission to use many of her stories from India, where she and her husband, Ron, have given years of faithful service.

The stories in this book are grouped by continents or areas—Africa, Asia, the Pacific Islands, etc. The first group of stories are some personal experiences from my own life of God's amazing care and power. Above all else, I thank God for His gracious kindness in opening the way for a Canadian farmer's son to have the privilege of taking part in global evangelism in more than fifty countries during the past thirty years.

James H. Zachary
November 2002

CONTENTS

PREFACE

Hitherto the Lord hath led! What a joy in these pages to read how God is personally interested and active in the here and now of daily human life!

God's timing in answering prayer may be immediate (as when Elijah prayed for fire on Mount Carmel) or after real or apparent setbacks (as when Daniel was carried to Babylon as a captive). Sometimes answers may come—as illustrated in Jesus' resurrection—after a restful three-day sleep. Yet God's answers to our prayers will always be better, though at times different, than we imagined.

Satan was not incorrect in saying that God had placed a hedge around Job (see Job 1:9, 10). God places such a hedge about each of His children. Real and threatened breaks do occur in that hedge for various reasons, yet always God is there, bending over us with compassion, ready to listen and answer when we call.

It has been my joy to have Pastor Jim Zachary as a friend and to thrill at his accounts of God's personal workings around this earth. In the spotlight here is not the storyteller, nor the subjects of the stories, but the God who answers prayer. Today, as much as in Bible times, He is still a God who cares for us and who answers our prayers.

Come read. Then go, taste and see that He is good!

Gayle R. Wilson, M.D.

HANDS IN THE DARK

"The flood took out the bridge. There will be no train for months. If you need a place to stay, there is an inn across the river on that hill," the passing man counseled Jack at the train station in a village in Canada.

Jack stepped out of the tiny waiting room and headed for the inn. It was almost midnight. The young literature evangelist picked up a stick as he approached the flooded river, which was flowing over the bridge. Feeling his way by striking the bridge surface with his stick, he crossed the river. As he stepped onto land, a large log struck the bridge and skidded over the top.

He stared into the darkness of the moonless night. Ahead he saw a light. As he approached, he saw it was the back of a restaurant. Knocking on the door, he could hear voices inside. Again he knocked. Suddenly the door opened, and a drunken man with a knife stood before him. Jack felt the pressure of the knife against his jacket as the man threatened him. Then he suddenly turned away and shut the door.

What should Jack do? Looking higher he saw another light. Praying that it was coming from the inn, he began to walk toward the light. He climbed a hill that was muddy from the rain. Soon he found himself stumbling over a rough stony area. After several minutes of climbing, he reached a level surface. His spirits lifted; the light was nearer now, and the climb was nearly over.

Suddenly he felt two hands grasp his shoulders and pull him backward. "Who's there?" he called, thinking of the drunken man. There was no response. He could not feel the person who had taken hold of him. *What is in front of me?* he thought. Now on his knees he felt for the surface of the ground in front of him. There was nothing there! Finally he found a small stone and gave it a toss. There was no sound. Thinking that the stone must have rolled into some mud, he picked up a second stone. As Jack was about to throw it, he heard, far below, the faint splash of the first stone.

Now he knew that his guardian angel had held him from falling to his death. Hearing voices, he saw the lights of miners changing shifts. At his call, they waited for him. They told him that an abandoned mine shaft 2,000 feet deep lay open behind him.

This experience happened to Jack, my father, while he was still single. I thank the Lord for that angel. My four sisters and I owe our lives to his intervention. We look forward to the day when we shall meet him face-to-face and thank him for saving the life of our father.

MORE THAN SIXTY YEARS OF EVANGELISM

I praise God for *The Quiet Hour*. In 1970, Jean and I left California and began eighteen precious years of missionary work. It was in the Philippines where I first experienced the encouraging help of *The Quiet Hour*.

We were assigned as professors at Mountain View College, a missionary school. Each weekend, students and teachers hike to distant villages to assist in the worship services and to conduct public and personal evangelism.

A letter was written to *The Quiet Hour* requesting help with transportation for the evangelistic outreach. What a wonderful day it was when Elder L. E. Tucker arrived to dedicate the six used military weapons carriers, which had been converted into buses for evangelism! Now the students could reach out even farther. During the next six years, the students planted forty new churches with the help of their transportation system.

The church grows when the entire membership is involved in sharing Jesus with the community. But villagers had a difficult time supplying materials for the new and enlarged church buildings. Often the members went into the jungle to cut trees for construction. *The Quiet Hour* frequently provided sheets of metal roofing.

Then there was the day when the Manobo tribal chief asked for teachers to come to his village. This animist tribe had only a handful of members who had even minimal reading skills. What a blessing when funds from *The Quiet Hour* listeners made it possible to send teachers into several remote jungle villages. Today, more than 3,000 of these people are now followers of Jesus. Again, thanks to the ministry of *The Quiet Hour*.

Following my six years at Mountain View, I spent three years as a professor at the theological seminary near Manila. The most effective type of training is by demonstration, so a citywide evangelistic program for Manila was organized. We needed Bibles. A letter was written once again to *The Quiet Hour*. "Can you help us with 100,000 Bibles?" was our request. Church members in Manila prayed for those Bibles, which were to be used in the outreach of 300 small groups. The day the letter arrived in Redlands a special prayer was offered for Bibles. Before the day was over, a *Quiet Hour* supporter called to say, "I feel impressed that you can use funds for Bibles." This dear sister pledged $50,000 for Bibles. The Holy Spirit touched the hearts of hundreds of supporters. In four months the Bibles were ordered. What a wonderful day when church leaders in Manila unloaded the hundreds of boxes containing the 100,000 Bibles! On the final day of the public meeting, 1,500 people were baptized. In the weeks that followed, hundreds more were baptized, and eleven new churches were formed.

UNDER HIS WINGS

During my academy days, my father had moved the family to a farm near Oshawa Missionary College in Canada. Days were spent between the classroom and caring for the farm. Everyone helped. My four sisters and I learned how to work.

Family worship was always a part of the start of a new day for the family. Dad would read a portion of Scripture or a page or two from a Spirit of Prophecy book and then lift his voice in prayer to God.

One day I was hoeing a field of vegetables. Dorene, my oldest sister, was cultivating an adjoining field with a spring-tooth cultivator. This field was being prepared for sowing a new crop. The cultivator was being pulled by three horses hitched up to a three-horse evener.

Molly was the family favorite. This horse was a delight to work with. While cultivating endless rows of corn, Molly would turn into the next row without any guidance. For my sister Dorene, Molly was easy to guide.

Suddenly I heard a noise. As I turned, I noticed that the tongue of the cultivator had dropped out of the ring on the yoke. As the wooden beam struck Molly's feet, she began to run. By the time I saw them, the three horses were at a full gallop.

Dorene was clinging to the metal seat. The reins had fallen to the ground. I knew my sister could fall under the cultivator at any moment. She seemed seconds away from death or serious injury.

"Dear Lord, help me," I prayed. The reins had fallen under the cultivator. The horses were galloping in a large circle. I ran toward the runaway team. Taking hold of a bridle I brought the horses to a stop. Dorene was still clinging to the seat. We thanked God for His protection as we unhitched the horses from the broken cultivator.

GOD HEARS AND ANSWERS PRAYER

The most precious gift parents can pass on to their children is a strong faith in God. I thank the Lord that my parents displayed a strong faith in their daily lives. One incident stands out in my mind. It was during the Great Depression. My father had lost his little business. The family had nowhere to turn for help.

After considerable prayer my parents decided that they had to leave our home in a small village and move to a city where Dad hoped to find employment. The move was made, and Dad began to search for work.

It wasn't long before all his savings were gone. We did not meet the minimum residence requirements to receive welfare. The picture is still very vivid in my mind. Our family was seated at the table. Mother had opened the last can of food and sliced the last loaf of bread. The cupboard was empty.

We sat around in semi-darkness early one morning. Dad did not have the funds to pay for electric power, so our electricity had been cut off. We bowed our heads in prayer. Dad prayed simply, "Dear Father, thank You for the tomatoes and bread. You know, Lord, that this is all the food we have. Please provide food for our lunch and supper today. In Jesus' name, Amen."

Mother placed a small portion on each plate of the seven family members, and we started to eat. There was a knock at the door. In his small-town manner, Dad called out, "Please, come in." The door opened. I saw the silhouette of a man as he stood in the doorway. He stood there for a few moments taking in the picture of the morning meal. He said nothing, closed the door, and left.

An hour later he returned. He brought with him a bushel basket filled with food. Within an hour my father's prayer was answered. Right on the top of the bushel was a large ham. Mother thanked the Lord for the ham. She traded it for a goodly supply of potatoes. I knew then, as I do now, that God hears and answers prayer.

LEST WE FORGET

As I travel from country to country, I have been touched by the conditions in which many of our believers live and work. Recently, I sat in a church filled with worshipers. But no church workers were present; they were imprisoned for their faith. The Bibles the members so reverently held were smuggled into the country, for the government does not permit the publishing of religious literature.

In another country, I visited a little house on the edge of a city. Each Sabbath, church members secretly entered the house to worship; they sang in whispers to prevent detection.

Then one day police raided the house and arrested the pastor. He remains in prison.

In another country, I met an elderly man sitting by himself in church. When he had refused to send his children to school on Sabbath, the authorities took his children and sent them to a communist boarding school. Today the children are atheists. Only God knows the depth of this man's sorrow.

I visited a Christian community service leader who cannot preach in a church or even make a comment during Bible study time, for religion is monitored where he serves.

In yet another country, a Christian pastor's home was bombed by a radical religious group. In spite of fear for his family, he continues to preach the gospel.

A teenager came to evangelistic meetings, her face and arms covered with bruises. Her father had beaten her to discourage her from accepting Jesus. One night as she returned from a Christian meeting, her father met her and tried to drag her to the barn for another whipping. She clung to a water pipe. Her father gave a violent yank, and the water pipe broke. He forgot the whipping as he repaired the broken pipe. Today, this young woman rejoices in the Lord in spite of persecution.

I stepped into a pastor's one-room apartment in another country. A bare light bulb hung in the center of the room. The pastor knelt on the floor beside his bed, preparing a Bible study. I prayed that, for his safety, the police had not seen me enter the apartment. It would have been far too dangerous to visit the secret house-church. Yet, this godly pastor and his family serve the Lord.

Unsung heroes live and work in many dark and dangerous places around the world. They are determined to serve God at any cost. We must pray for those who are suffering for the Lord, and we must never take our religious freedom for granted.

SAVED BY AN ANGEL

Jack and Viva Zachary always gathered their five children together for family worship, even during the busy days of sowing and harvest time on the farm. Every member of the family helped in the field.

It was time for the hay to be brought in and stacked to provide for the cattle and horses during the long Canadian winters. The family lacked today's modern machinery, so there was a great deal of hand work. As soon as the hay was mowed and dried properly, the hard work of bringing it into the hay loft began.

After a hearty breakfast, my father, sisters, and I headed for the hay field. We climbed on the empty wagon for the ride to the hayfield. The horses were guided to pull the wagon between two rows of hay that had been raked into long windrows.

Dad and I picked up forkfuls of hay and placed them on the wagon. My sisters had been trained in how to move the fork loads of hay to properly load the hay wagon. In about thirty minutes Dad and I were lifting the hay almost ten feet to the top of the load.

The load was pulled into the barn. A large fork was forced into the hay, and the clamp tightened. The fork load of hay was lifted into the barn and dropped into the hay mow.

One day we had completed the task of loading the wagon when I heard one of my sisters cry out in fear. I remembered that she was at the front of the wagon. She had been standing near Molly. Molly was a horse that had been used for many years to pull the family plow and cultivator. Pulling the wagon was a different matter. When Molly felt the back straps hit her on her rump, she was ready to kick or run.

My sister had fallen toward Molly. As I ran to the front of the wagon, she was hanging on to the hay just inches from Molly's back. I took hold of my sister and lifted her to the ground before she could touch Molly's rump.

What was holding my sister from landing on Molly's back, only to be kicked and run over by the wagon? I knew that the hay around a newly loaded wagon was loose. I reached up with my fork. Considerable hay fell to the ground at my touch.

That night at family worship we all prayed, thanking God for sparing the life of Delores.

PRAISE GOD, WE ARE FREE!

A large crowd gathered on the edge of the community swimming pool in Addis Ababa, Ethiopia to witness a baptism of nearly 300 new Christians. Pastor Truneh Wolde-Selassie, Ethiopian Union president, his eyes shining with tears, whispered emotionally, "It is wonderful, wonderful!"

This baptism signaled a new day for the work in Ethiopia. It was the first public baptism held in the eighty-six-year history of the church there. Until recently, opposition from the national church and the communist government has prevented public meetings and baptisms.

Pastor Truneh told how his village had been destroyed by a religious mob when he was twelve years old. He watched as two church leaders were shot; then the gun was pointed at his father. Suddenly a man leaped forward and pushed the gun aside, shouting, "Two deaths are enough." Several months before, Truneh's father had saved this man's life when he was seriously ill.

The mob set fire to the village, and the group of terrified Christians fled to the mission office with only the clothes they wore. The fire lighted their path as they walked into the night.

Restrictions and persecution made evangelism difficult. Baptisms were held secretly at night. A group of communists discovered one secret baptism and tried to "baptize" the pastor. But God protected him, and he escaped their efforts to drown him.

God richly blessed the Addis Ababa public meeting. Seventeen cottage meetings have been held under the direction of Filipino pastor Edwin Gulfan, a Bible teacher at an Ethiopian Christian college. The crowd in the open-air stadium grew each night from 1,500 to 3,000. As the meeting closed, 596 persons were baptized, and more than 700 joined the baptismal classes.

Pastor Truneh commented, "At last we are free. We must work while we have the opportunity." Hundreds of small groups prepared the way for a great harvest of souls in a nationwide evangelistic effort in 1996. Pray for Ethiopia, its faithful workers, and the new believers there.

COURAGEOUS MISSIONARY

As Rupelin Gorospe and her three young children boarded the aircraft for the Philippines, she turned to those who had come to see her off. "I will return and carry on the work that my husband and I started," she promised.

Rupelin and Art Gorospe had served as nurses in a remote clinic in Ethiopia before they transferred to a Christian college to serve the medical needs of students and staff. The hours in the clinic of the college were long. They needed time to relax.

The couple loaded their camping gear and their family into their little car and drove out of town for a weekend of relaxation. As the family car turned off the main road, a man with a gun blocked their way. He raised the gun and began firing into the car. Art and the family's maid died instantly. The children crouched in the car. When they began to move, the gunman fired again, but Rupelin and the children were not hit.

Anger and rage filled the hearts of the family's friends and co-workers when they learned what had happened. The killer took the lives of two innocent people and got only the family's picnic lunch.

Rupelin went to the police, not to demand justice but to plead for the life of the killer. "Please, when you find this man, spare his life. I forgive him." The killer, a man named Kabato, was eventually arrested and is in prison. A friend of Art Gorospe, fellow missionary Chris Howell, visited Kabato and told him of Rupelin's plea for his life. Howell studied with Kabato, who eventually accepted Jesus as his Savior and was baptized.

After several weeks of mourning in the Philippines, Rupelin Gorospe returned to Ethiopia and her duties as the college nurse, meeting the medical needs of the sick in the community as well as the college.

Life is hard in the college community. Two years ago, another teacher was murdered. Recently, angry people from the community attempted to burn the house of the college treasurer. He resigned his position and left the city.

But Rupelin is a courageous young woman; she and her children are staying on. The people need her help. Hers is the spirit that will carry the gospel to the world in spite of challenges and difficulties.

Pray earnestly and continually for the missionaries and evangelists such as Rupelin who minister for Jesus on the front lines.

"GIVE ME A HARD PLACE TO WORK"

The evangelism team had just arrived in Ghana. As we entered the crowded motel, we thanked God for the air conditioner that helped to relieve the tropical heat. Suddenly, the electricity failed, the water stopped flowing, and the cool air ceased. The tiny motel rooms became sweat boxes. One volunteer, a wealthy woman, lamented, "Why did I ever come?"

The team faced a big challenge: Its target community was mostly Muslim, where evangelism was difficult and discouraging. Earnestly, the team prayed for the Lord's help. But even before they could pray, the Lord was answering their prayers.

A Muslim man in the city faced great problems in his business and his family. Five times a day he spread out his prayer mat and asked Allah for help, but he received no answers. Then one night he dreamed he saw Jesus kindly, lovingly beckoning him to come.

As he awakened he thought, *If Jesus is so kind, why not ask Him for help?* So he prayed. And one by one, his prayers were being answered. What joy!

Another day the man dreamed he watched a parade. Marchers held placards that discouraged smoking and drinking and a sign that advertised a Health Expo evangelistic meeting. In his dream someone handed him a handbill.

Two days later he watched as a parade passed his business. He recognized it as the parade he had seen in his dream. A person handed him a piece of paper. It was the same handbill he had seen in his dream! He decided that Allah must surely want him at this meeting!

He attended the meetings regularly. When the evangelist gave the invitation to follow Jesus, this Muslim man was the first to stand. Others followed his example. This experience brought encouragement to the evangelistic team, especially to the wealthy woman. She exclaimed, "I want to come back again! And please send me to a hard place!"

God would like to use each member of the world church as a witness to those searching for His help. As we submit our lives to His guidance, God will use us to help win others to Himself.

FAITHFUL UNDER PERSECUTION

Hannah Ramatu stood in the shadows, a safe distance from the evangelist's tent. A good Muslim would not be seen here, but she wanted to hear the health lectures, and she enjoyed the music.

She stayed to hear the pastor's message and found she knew some of the Bible characters mentioned—Abraham and the prophet Jesus. One evening, as the pastor described the death of Jesus, the Holy Spirit convicted her heart. "Jesus died for *me!*" The thought overwhelmed her; she *had* to learn more about Jesus! Before the meetings ended, Hannah decided to follow Christ.

Hannah's father was outraged. How could his daughter commit this great sin of becoming a Christian? A struggle ensued. First he burned her Bible to bring Hannah to her senses. Then he had her hair cut off to remove the evil that "infected" her soul. But she remained faithful to her new Friend, Jesus.

Then he sent Hannah to her Muslim uncle's home with instructions to confine her to his house. He hoped that, away from her Christian friends, she would forget her new faith. However, another Christian preacher was conducting evangelistic meetings near her uncle's home, and Hannah listened from her window! She thanked God for strengthening her in this way.

When she returned home, more sure of her faith then ever, Hannah's father threatened to kill her. This was no idle threat. He was the village butcher! Hannah fled to the mission headquarters. Church leaders went to visit Hannah's father. On their way, villagers tried to stone their car.

When Hannah returned home, her father beat her with a horse whip. Her arms and back were covered with blood. Desperate, Hannah ran to the local police for protection. The police told Hannah's father, "Your daughter is an adult now, free to choose her own religion. You will be in trouble if you harm her."

Hannah is living at home, learning to become a seamstress. Her parents no longer force her to deny her faith. Hannah knows that there is no greater freedom than living in the presence of Jesus, who freed her from sin. Hannah is free indeed!

"JESUS LOVES YOU"

The government official pushed a security button. A guard appeared. "Take this man out of my office," the official ordered. The young preacher stood and walked to the door where the guard waited. At the door, he turned back and said to the official, "Abdul, Jesus loves you." In spite of the harsh way he had been treated, he added, "Abdul, I will come back to visit you. And remember, Jesus loves you."

Abdul hated both the name of Jesus and the Bible, but he could not push those words out of his mind.

In 1982 the preacher returned and went to the same government office. "Abdul, I have come to personally invite you to come to my meeting tonight." Abdul promised that he would come.

He gathered some of his friends to assist him. "Tonight, we will destroy this preacher and many of his followers," he told them. He hid a hand grenade in his clothing as he left for the meeting. He seated himself where he would be able to kill the largest number of people along with the pastor. After some singing, the young preacher stepped forward. Abdul returned the preacher's smile. "This will be the last time he will smile," Abdul said to himself.

The preacher was telling a story from Mark 10—the story of blind Bartimaeus. As Abdul listened to the story, the preacher looked directly at him. It seemed as if he himself were the blind man. The preacher described Bartimaeus's asking about the meaning of the shuffling feet on the path. "Jesus of Nazareth is passing by," the people told him. Then the blind man called to Jesus for help. Looking straight at Abdul, the preacher said, "You must call on Jesus today. You are the one sitting by the roadside."

Abdul felt something happening to him. His legs were shaking. His hair felt strange. His mind was astir. "I am sitting by the roadside. I need this Jesus," he whispered to himself.

The sermon continued, "Bartimaeus called to Jesus. And Jesus turned around and said 'Come to Me.' " The preacher took a step closer to Abdul and said, "Come." Then in louder voice, and looking directly at Abdul, he repeated, "Come! Jesus is calling you. Come!" Later, Abdul said, "I could feel something like a loud gong sounding in my heart. I found myself standing up, and I started to move forward."

Abdul's friends took hold of his clothes, "What are you doing? Where are you going?"

"Don't you hear?" Abdul replied. "Someone is calling me. Jesus Christ is calling me. I have to go." Abdul took off his Islamic cap and gown as he moved forward toward the preacher. His friends were amazed to see their leader changing his plan of action. They all got up and left.

The next day Abdul's father, along with a number of his powerful friends, visited Abdul's office. His father led the way. He took out a knife as the group said, "Kill him! Kill him!" Abdul remembered that the night before some of the people at the meeting had told him, "If you have any trouble, call upon the name of Jesus."

As his father advanced toward him and placed a knife at his neck, Abdul said, "Father, before you kill me, please give me time to pray." He prayed, "Lord Jesus, this is my last moment. Heavenly Father, in the name of Jesus, I pray that my father's knife will be taken away." Abdul felt a mighty power as his father slowly backed away. Joining his friends, the father said, "He is mad. Let us leave him alone." Turning to Abdul he said, "You are going to lose your job, your home, everything."

Although he used to have a high position and a place in a wealthy family, today Abdul receives only $100.00 per month as he shares his faith in Jesus. He is often persecuted as he publicly tells audiences of the power of Jesus. But his burden is to reach his Islamic friends with the good news of the power of Jesus to save sinners.

A STREET CHILD FINDS GOD

When he was two months old, George was given to his grandmother to rear. Upon her death, his care fell to his grandmother's sister. When life became unbearable, George ran away; he was only nine years old. For five years he lived on the streets of Nairobi. He has never met his parents. "I tried to find something to eat from the garbage cans. I begged near the stop signs, and it was good when people gave me money for food," George recalls.

Then something happened that turned George's life around. One of the Pathfinder clubs from Nairobi was having an outing in a local city park. The children wanted to find some street children and help them. Each Pathfinder brought along three extra lunches so they could eat together with the street urchins.

The club went to the section of town where there were many street children. They personally invited these children to join their outing. The Pathfinder club led their guests to the Jeervrjee Garden. The program began with a spiritual talk. Some of the children had never heard about Jesus before. Club members invited the forty children from the street to join in several games.

George was one of the children who happened to be near the city park looking for food in the garbage bins when the Pathfinders showed up. He admired their uniforms and came closer out of curiosity. Soon they invited him to join the fun. How good it was to get a good meal from one of the Pathfinders! After the meal, there was singing and more games.

As the exciting party drew to a close, George made a request, "I wish that I could become a Pathfinder too." When he was asked why he wanted to be a Pathfinder, he replied, "I want to be like these children and go to school." The Pathfinder leader made a promise, "I will return to the park in two days. Please meet me here."

The leader called the Adventist school to see whether they would accept George as a boarding student. George, now fourteen, had not completed the fourth grade. Life was so different at the school. Good food replaced the scraps from the garbage cans. He didn't have to find a place on the sidewalk to sleep, and he didn't have to run when the police came by.

"I'm happy now," George says. "Life is good. I'm able to go to school now." George has joined the baptismal class.

THE JOY OF CHRIST

Dennis Patinde pastors a small group of Christians in Mali, a predominantly Muslim country.

Lamine is the son of the imam, the Muslim teacher. From childhood Lamine had memorized large portions of the Qu'ran. But as he matured, he became discouraged over the uncertainties of life. He wished for a deeper spiritual experience, but he did not know how to achieve it. Then he met Pastor Patinde, the first Christian pastor Lamine had ever known. "Religion should be a joy," Lamine told Patinde. "So why is it such a burden? Why is there so much fear and hatred, so much killing?"

The youthful pastor and the imam's son talked for some time. As the two discussed spiritual issues and prayed together, Lamine caught a new glimpse of God. Patinde gave Lamine a Bible, and Lamine began to read it. He was amazed that it contained some stories found in the Qu'ran.

When Lamine read in the Qu'ran that a true believer should read the Torah, the prophets, the Injil (Gospels), and other writings of the Bible, he felt that he was following the counsel of Mohammed, Islam's prophet. As he continued studying the Bible, his burden was replaced with joy. He felt a peace he had never known.

Lamine had to be careful that no one saw him enter or leave the pastor's home. Each night he went home by a different route so that no one would know where he had been.

But in spite of his care, word spread that Lamine, the son of the imam, had become a Christian. Lamine's parents were angry and disowned him. Pastor Patinde visited them and talked about their son. "Something has happened to our son," Lamine's father said. "He is a different boy; happy and confident." Patinde explained that Lamine had discovered the joy of salvation in Jesus Christ.

Lamine's parents eventually accepted his new faith and are now studying the Bible. Lamine is praying that they, too, will follow Jesus one day soon.

AN ORPHAN USED BY GOD

Immaculee was born in Gitarama town in Rwanda. Her parents were poisoned when she was less than two months old. Her older sister took care of her. Through her childhood she felt that all people were evil. She often feared for her life.

While in Catholic primary school, Immaculee decided to follow God. She was impressed by the loving care of the nuns in her school and decided to become a sister. However, because she was uneducated, they refused to accept her in the convent.

Discouraged, she often slipped alone into the forest. She often spent days in prayer asking God for help. She began to fellowship with a Pentecostal group. As she watched her Pentecostal friends associating with their parents, she and her sister became more lonely and discouraged. She longed for a family.

One day in desperation Immaculee prayed, "God please show up today. If You don't help me, I don't want to live any longer." As she prayed, she felt something like a shock of electricity. "I thought, 'Now I have received the Spirit as the Pentecostal pastor taught.' "

At this time Immaculee was invited to attend an Adventist small-group prayer session. She was impressed by the joy of the members in the little group. She was curious about their statements regarding the joy they found in worshiping God on the Sabbath. Immaculee slipped into the forest again and spent six days fasting and praying for God to help her to find happiness and to learn what the Sabbath is.

She became convinced that she must join this happy group. The next Sabbath she attended the Adventist church. It seemed to the young woman that the church members received her as their daughter. "Now I have parents and a family," she felt. For the first time in her life Immaculee was happy.

Her former church people were circulating stories that she was attending the Adventist church to find a husband. She returned to the Pentecostal church and requested that she be permitted to give her testimony. They said, "The Spirit has shown us that our lamb would return." Immaculee decided that theirs was not the true spirit or they would know that she was determined to become a Sabbath keeper.

All of her life Immaculee had felt a great burden of guilt for her sins. Upon reading *The Desire of Ages*, she discovered a close relationship with Jesus and felt the peace of God as she repented of her sins. She now was the only Adventist in Gitarama.

Immaculee began to share her new joy with her neighbors. She shared the Bible truths she had learned in her baptismal class. She soon had a little company of seven Sabbath keepers. As the group grew, Immaculee knew that a church building was needed. She visited neighboring churches requesting assistance for her growing group of believers. Church members made the dried-mud bricks, and ADRA provided the metal roofing. She did have one problem. Church members made doors and windows from donated wood. However, before they could be installed thieves took them. In spite of this, Immaculee praised God that there now was a church building in her village even though the doors and windows were missing.

In 2002, the company of more than 100 members was organized into a church in Gitarama with Immaculee serving as one of the elders.

"I'm very happy now because Jesus has given me happiness in my heart. Jesus is coming soon, and we will see the harvest of the people we have been working for," she testified. Immaculee accepts invitations to preach in churches and has preached in more than twenty public evangelistic meetings throughout southern Rwanda. Immaculee has no idea how many souls the Lord has given her. She praises God that her meetings have resulted in new companies of believers being formed.

SOWING GOSPEL SEED

Marguerite is a widow; her husband passed away in the 1970s. During the 1994 genocide, she lost her son and son-in-law. She and her widowed daughter have adopted three young people orphaned by the genocide. She now lives in Nyanza.

A Bible verse gave a clear direction for her life. Jesus said, "The kingdom of God is as if a man should scatter seed on the ground, and should sleep by night and rise by day, and the seed should sprout and grow, he himself does not know how. For the earth yields crops by itself: first the blade, then the head, after that the full grain in the head. But when the grain ripens, immediately he puts in the sickle, because the harvest has come" (Mark 4:26-29, NKJV).

Marguerite began sowing gospel seed, and the Lord has richly blessed her efforts. While still employed by World Vision in Kigali, she spent her vacation time in evangelism around Nyanza city in the south of Rwanda. At her own expense she made the long trip by bus. Her first evangelism program was conducted in Cyaraksi. A couple of women helped make personal calls on villagers, inviting them to attend the meeting. Marguerite secured some booklets to use as gifts. She did the preaching. She rejoiced to see fifty persons accept the gospel.

Marguerite was greatly inspired that a widow could be so richly blessed by the Lord. She determined to continue sowing seed. This was the first of the thirty-four evangelistic meetings she has conducted. Over the years she has borne the majority of the expense for these meetings.

Seeing the great need for church buildings for her converts, Marguerite visited several congregations requesting financial assistance. Little by little construction was started on a church at Gahande. While her team was able to make their own mud/straw bricks, the cost of the roof was beyond their reach. Marguerite had to wait three years to take her turn in receiving metal roofing through Global Mission funding. The South Rwanda Association currently is waiting for roofs for seventy churches. It is urgent that this need be filled soon. The rainy season destroys the dried-mud walls. Some congregations have had to rebuild their churches three times while waiting for a roof.

After World Vision cut back on staff, Marguerite began earning her living as a literature evangelist. She now lives in Nyanza, closer to her field of labor. Each weekend she visits her converts and preaches in her churches. With God's special blessing Marguerite has constructed three churches to accommodate her converts.

A THOUSAND SHALL FALL AT THY SIDE

Samuel formerly earned his living by selling grain and other farm products. Currently he spends almost all his time in evangelism.

During the time of the genocide in 1994, the Lord protected Samuel in a marvelous way. His name did not appear on the lists of persons who were to be exterminated. There were seven persons who asked if they could be hidden in his house. Several of the seven were women. His own wife's name appeared on the fearful list.

The soldiers discovered that he was protecting wanted people. Two soldiers were sent to search his home. Samuel prayed for God to protect his wife and guests. "It is a mystery," Samuel says, "the soldiers did not see the people in my home." Samuel's house is very small. He can only thank God that the soldiers were blinded somehow by God so they saw only two persons whose names were not on the list. It was a miracle that the lives of the others were spared.

Still others were looking for a safe place of refuge. Samuel pleaded with God for help in hiding people. One night he looked out his window and saw a captain of the army coming to him. "You know that I am a military man, a captain in the army. Do not be afraid, I am not coming to kill anyone. I am an angel of the Lord."

The captain stayed with Samuel until the killing was over. "This is a mystery that I cannot fully explain. During this terrible time I lost no family member to death. The refugees in my home all survived." Each time Samuel shares this experience he thanks God for His care.

At times some of the refugees decided that they would attempt to escape to a nearby country. Samuel urged them to stay. "I told them that God was the One who was sending His angels to protect them." He often quoted the scripture that speaks of thousands falling but that death would not come to the faithful. They all decided to stay. Not one of his refugees perished.

Today Samuel is an outstanding lay preacher. It all started in 1986 when he developed a burden for those who were backsliding. He preached in many churches. "It became a new way of life for me," Samuel testifies. Since the time of the genocide, Samuel has conducted from four to five two-week evangelistic meetings each year.

During one of his meetings in 1997, in Butare, the home base of Catholicism for the entire nation, he faced a new challenge. As the second week started, he had fifty-three persons who had requested baptism. When the religious authorities discovered the plans for the baptism, they complained to the police. The police department confiscated all his evangelistic equipment. Samuel had to stop preaching. His fifty-three converts told Samuel, "You can't leave us without baptizing us. The truth you have taught has touched our hearts." The mayor told the police to return all the confiscated equipment. Samuel then faced a new problem. A search of the city and nearby communities showed that there was no water for a baptism. He had to rent taxis to take them to another city. Soon Samuel had 650 members attending a new company in Butare.

On another occasion, Samuel was preparing to preach before 300 persons. A snake came from behind. He wondered how he could defend himself. "God helped me to pick up a stick and stop the snake from attacking me," he said. What a dramatic way to begin a meeting! The people seemed drawn out night after night. Eventually, 125 persons decided for baptism. Now Samuel needed a church.

He gathered the converts and started to make dried-mud bricks. Before the rainy season began they had constructed all the walls. There were no funds to purchase the metal sheets for the roof. The $2,000 for the roof was impossible for the members to raise. From week to week they met in a scanty shelter covered with scraps of plastic and cloth. The heavy rains caused the mud bricks to crumble. When the rains had stopped, the walls were down. Without a complaint, they started the building process all over.

The local mission has seventy church buildings that are waiting for a metal sheet roof. During the three-year period, several have had to be reconstructed in the hopes that their church would be next in line for a roof.

TWO STUDENTS USED BY GOD

Seven hundred Adventist students attend the public university in Butari, Rwanda. There is no Adventist church located in Butari. Seventy-five percent of the population belongs to the Catholic Church, and Butari serves as the denomination's center for the nation. The university allows the Adventist college youth to conduct their Sabbath services in the stadium.

Nyira Mutufo Posealine and her friend, Irene Ribakare, were in their senior year. Together they enrolled in a class that was required for graduation. Rwanda follows the French system of education in which the final exam is the sole evaluation of the students' work. If one did not sit for that examination, the entire year's work would be lost.

While the majority of the Rwandan professors were understanding of Sabbath problems, many times guest professors from Europe were not.

The two Adventist girls were told that their examination for this particular class would fall on a Sabbath. On Wednesday of the examination week, they visited with the guest professor. "Sir, we are members of the Seventh-day Adventist Church. Saturday is the Bible Sabbath. Can you arrange to have us sit for the examination on another day?" they asked.

The answer was abrupt and a bit harsh. "No, you must take the examination with the others."

The two girls spent a lot of time in prayer. Friendly students sympathized with their problem. "Surely your God will understand. You ought to take the exam."

On Friday the girls visited with their professor again. This time he was even harsher in rejecting their request. "There will be no exceptions," he told them. "You must appear for the exam. This is final."

As they discussed their problem that evening, they made their decision. "Even if we lose this entire year, we will not take the exam. We will retake this year's study next year."

Early Sabbath morning, they took a hike into the nearby forest. They spent several hours in prayer. They prayed until it was time to go to the stadium for Sabbath School and church.

Their fellow students appeared for the examination at 8:00 A.M. The professor was not present. The minutes passed as the students waited. At 10:00 a teacher appeared and informed the students that the copies of the examination could not be located. The exam would be rescheduled.

As the girls left church, their classmates said, "Your God must love you very much. The examination has been rescheduled."

THE RUNAWAY

Stephen grew up in a Christian home in Bangladesh. His parents sent him to a Christian school where he could grow in his knowledge of Christ. But Stephen took the spiritual environment for granted and put off making a decision for Christ. After he graduated, he studied in a government school where he soon forgot the lessons he had learned in the Christian school. He eventually turned from God and married one of his classmates.

Stephen borrowed money to start a business, but when his business collapsed, he ran from his creditors, neglecting his family responsibilities. As his life crumbled, Stephen remembered the peace he had known in a Christian environment. He recalled the teachings he had learned but never appreciated. He thought about the close walk with Jesus he could have had.

While still in hiding, Stephen heard of Sathsumila, a Christian training center in Bangladesh that trains lay volunteers to plant churches. Stephen enrolled in some classes. At Sathsumila Stephen gave his life to God for service. He determined to make amends for his past mistakes and to be a good husband and father. He sent for his family to join him.

In the school Stephen reviewed the teachings of Christianity. He learned how to reach non-Christians with the gospel, how to help people to stop smoking, and how to conduct small-group evangelism.

After he completed his studies, Stephen accepted a call to work in two non-Christian communities in Bangladesh. He made friends with the villagers, helping them in their gardens and teaching them ways to improve their health. He has helped many villagers stop smoking and has organized three small village groups for Bible study.

As a result of Stephen's first series of Bible studies, he led eleven people to accept the Lord. He hopes to plant a church in each village and to construct a small clinic to help with the medical needs of the villagers. After years of running from God, Stephen feels that he is finally where God wants him to be.

A REFUGEE FINDS HOPE IN JESUS

During Pol Pot's regime, Cambodians were taken from cities and forced to labor under impossible conditions. Starvation and death were common. Hardly a family escaped without losing at least one member. Iam Wet lost his parents, sister, brother, and more than thirty members of his extended family. Soon he realized that his only hope for survival lay in escaping his homeland. He joined the thousands who risked being shot as they made their way toward the safety of the Thai border.

Iam made it across the border and spent the next seventeen years living in a refugee camp in Thailand. He married and fathered four children while in the camp.

The camps were full of people desperate to find lost relatives. As families fled Cambodia, they often became separated attempting to avoid soldiers. For eight years Iam worked with the Red Cross trying to locate lost family members. Every day he met death and sorrow face-to-face, and eventually he lost hope in the future.

Raised a Buddhist, Iam accepted a friend's invitation to visit a Christian church. There—for the first time in his life—he heard the story of Jesus, who volunteered to die for the sins of the world. From that one visit Iam began to believe that there is a God—a God who cares for humanity.

As soon as it was safe to return to Phnom Penh, Iam enrolled his children in a public school. But he was concerned about the level of moral education they were receiving. A neighbor told him that an Adventist church had just opened a new school. She described the spiritual influence that the school offered. Iam transferred his children to this new "God school."

Iam discovered that the pastor of this Adventist church had been his friend in the refugee camp. Iam and his wife went to visit their old friend, Hang Dara. Soon the couple began studying the Bible with their pastor friend, and in 1999 they were baptized.

Today Iam rejoices in a new life that his family has found in Jesus. "Everyday we thank God for the happiness and hope that we now have. And we look forward to the day that He will come again."

THE GOD WHO SENDS RAIN

The Meitei people, who live in the hills of northern India, are still largely unreached with the gospel.

Ranjit Singh and his wife worked for several days to plant 2,500 cabbage plants in their garden. But as they worked, they noticed that some of the cabbage plants were beginning to wither. The ground was dry, and there was no sign of rain. Without rain there would be no harvest, and the family would face a difficult year.

The Singhs had lost faith in the gods they had called upon throughout their lives, but they did not know where to turn for help. Which of India's 300,000 gods would answer their prayer for rain to make their cabbages grow?

Then Mr. Singh recalled hearing someone say that the God of the Christians was all-powerful. He talked it over with his wife, and they decided to pray to this unseen God for rain. "If the God of the Christians hears our prayer and answers, then we will know that He is the true God," Mr. Singh told his wife. For the first time in their lives the couple poured out their hearts to God for help.

That night it rained. The next day, the couple stood in amazement when they realized that the rain had fallen only on their cabbage patch and nowhere else in the village. Mr. Singh did not hesitate; he set out to learn how he could become a follower of this powerful God who had answered their prayer. But his wife hesitated.

Mr. Singh found a Protestant pastor and asked him how he could become a Christian. The pastor baptized him that day, and Mr. Singh went home happy. But he did not know what it meant to be a Christian. What should a follower of God be doing? How should he worship? What did God expect of him?

Sometime later Mr. Singh met an Adventist pastor and asked him, "What does it mean to be a Christian?" Through a series of Bible studies, the pastor showed the couple what it meant to follow Christ. Both Mr. and Mrs. Singh were baptized.

The miraculous rainfall did not go unnoticed by others in their village. Many were deeply impressed and have shown a willingness to learn more about the God who can control the wind and the rain.

THE WIDOW'S MAID

A young woman named Prabha from the lower caste of India obtained a position as a housemaid to a wealthy widow woman. As she worked for her employer, she spent long hours at her tasks.

One day a group of robbers invaded the home of the widow. During the robbery, the widow woman was killed, and Prabha was locked in an inner room of the house. When the police arrived, they discovered the young woman alone in the house. They arrested Prabha for the murder and put her in jail.

For three years the young woman cried out to her village and family gods from the place of her incarceration. She was innocent of the charges, but no one would believe her. As the years passed with no answer, she became very discouraged.

The local church elders assigned two *Quiet Hour* volunteers to this non-Christian village. They began house-to-house visits. They offered to pray for the people. Between themselves they prayed that the Lord would open the way for the gospel of Jesus to be shared with the entire village.

During their visits in the village, the two volunteers heard about the innocent housemaid who had been so long in prison. They remembered that the Savior had instructed His people to visit those in prison. They determined to go see her.

During their visit to the prison they asked the young woman whether she would like to have them pray to Jesus for her release from prison. They told her of some of the wonderful things that Jesus had done to help people when He lived on earth.

"Please pray for me," Prabha replied. "There is no one to help me anymore." The two volunteers pleaded with God to free the young woman.

The very next day the police captured a group of robbers in the act of committing a robbery. Under questioning they admitted that they had killed the widow. Within hours the jailer received orders to free the housemaid. The story quickly spread through the village that the very next day after the Christians had prayed for Prabha, their prayer had been answered.

"Please tell me more about Jesus," Prabha requested. Her family joined in the Bible study. Other villagers, too, requested more information about Jesus.

Today there is a lovely *Quiet Hour* chapel in that village, and the housemaid has a new job. She has become a village Bible teacher. Her days are full as she goes from house to house teaching others about the Jesus who heard her cry for help and answered.

THE FIRE STORM

Most of us live in a world isolated from the tragedies that befall Christians in other lands. For several years increased violence against believers in some countries received little public notice until an evangelical missionary, Graham Staines, and his two young sons were burned alive in their jeep by a group of extremists early in 1999.

Adventists have not escaped the violence against believers. During a lay training program in a certain country in Asia, a young man named Samson related his story.

Samson comes from a village in the central part of his country. During evangelistic meetings he and his family learned about the Bible Sabbath and decided to follow the clear teaching of God's Word. The Christian community grew until one in every three villagers was a Christian. The non-Christians began to feel threatened. Who would control community politics?

Then one day concern boiled over into violence. Christians had to flee for their lives. Their livestock was stolen, and their homes were looted and set afire. Fifteen young believers who tried to resist their attackers were hacked to death. Their bodies were piled up in the village square, dowsed with gasoline, and set ablaze. Samson's church lost one member in the massacre.

The government arrested fifty-four persons, but the non-Christian majority had so many friends in high positions that soon all those who had been arrested were released on bail. For nine months the believers who fled the village lived as refugees in a distant village.

Samson and other believers have since returned to their village. They are attempting to start over, but it takes time to build a home, build up new flocks and herds, and establish a new farming routine. The believers pray that they can form new relationships among the many religious communities in the village. But that is difficult when they have watched some of their numbers die.

In spite of the terrorism, the church has continued to grow. It now has more than 110 members, with another eighty members in nearby villages.

It is so easy to become news-hardened. The pictures of tears, death, and suffering barely interrupt our busy schedules. Let's do our best to reach out in love and prayer on behalf of those who suffer for Christ's sake.

A SNAKE LEADS TO CHRIST

Neighbors in Adavaram, a village in India, were awakened by a scream in the middle of the night. Eighteen-year-old Lakshmi had gotten up to relieve herself. Leaving her husband sleeping, she bent over and exited the door of her humble home. She walked down a dark path toward the dry rice paddy located a few yards from her house.

Suddenly a snake wrapped itself around both of her legs. With her legs held tightly, she fell to the ground. Terrified, she screamed. Into her mind came the memory of a conversation she had recently had with a neighbor. The neighbor had told her that she had been learning stories of Jesus and His great power from a Christian relative in a distant village. For the first time in her life, Lakshmi prayed to Jesus, "Jesus, save me!" Instantly, the snake loosened its grasp and slithered away.

Lakshmi and her husband, Ramarao, a rickshaw driver, were not believers. Lakshmi's friend, Paidama, has relatives who are believers. This family lives five miles away. During visits to Paidama and her family, these relatives have shared their faith in the living God. Paidama learned to sing songs about Jesus. She shared with her friend, Lakshmi, what she had been learning.

The day after the snake attack, Pastor Vra Nkhiha visited the village of Adavaram. He invited the people to join a Bible class. When Lakshmi heard the hymns, she joined the group in study. During the gathering she told the group about her experience with the snake the day before. She was convinced that Jesus had saved her life. God became very real to her.

Lakshmi and Ramarao decided that they would give a gift to Jesus to show their appreciation. They donated a lot located next to their home for a chapel. A church group in Oregon donated the money to build a small church on this lot.

Lakshmi and Ramarao were among the first people of this village to be baptized. They are now active in their new church, and Lakshmi often leads the singers in the Christian songs she has learned to love.

TWO YOUNG WOMEN FIND CHRIST

One day Ashalath Mandal was in the market buying vegetables when she noticed a man selling twelve small books for one rupee. She liked to read and couldn't resist the bargain. Among the books was one titled, *Gospel Stories From the New Testament*. She was fascinated. Who was this Jesus Christ who could feed 5,000 people with only five loaves and two fish? She sought out a Christian church and began to attend. As a result, she accepted Jesus as her Savior.

When her family heard of her decision, they were very angry and chased her out of their house. She had no one now, and she cried to God everyday. People mocked her and hated her. She felt so alone, but she clung to Jesus Christ. Then one day a person in her village became seriously ill with a tumor and was expected to die.

"If your God is real, as you say He is, then prove it to us," the villagers demanded of Ashalath. "Pray to your God to heal this sickness." Ashalath was afraid, but she knew she must try. She went to the sick person's home and read some verses of Scripture and prayed for healing. Immediately, the tumor disappeared and the person became well! Soon, the whole village was asking questions about Jesus Christ. They are now open to the preaching of the gospel.

Muktha Maity is another young woman from the same community who lived with her widowed mother. Although an unbeliever, she attended a Christian prayer meeting with a friend. That day she witnessed something wonderful. A devil-possessed woman was brought to the meeting. The devil was speaking through her. The woman was very strong, and no one could control her. The people were all afraid to go near her.

Then the pastor came to the woman with the evil spirit and placed his hand on her head, praying for her in the name of Jesus Christ. As he prayed, the devil struggled with the woman, and then she fell to the ground unconscious. After the prayer, she awoke and asked for some water to drink. She was completely normal. Muktha Maity saw this with her own eyes and marveled what a powerful God Jesus Christ must be to do such a thing. "I must know more about Him," she told C. Sangchia, the lay preacher who was holding the meeting. She attended the remainder of the meetings and was baptized. She, too, was thrown out of her house, but she remained true to God and His truth and has determined to devote her life to witnessing to God's power and love.

MIRACLES ON A RAILWAY PLATFORM

On Sabbath morning the railway platform at Pachora is crowded and noisy as usual. Trains come and go, and coolies vie with one another to carry the luggage of passengers. Up and down the platform are vendors with their pushcarts, hawking their wares of fruits, snacks, cool drinks, and magazines. The place is a beehive of activity. But if you watch closely, you will see that some of those entering the platform do not carry luggage, but rather Bibles. They are all going to the far end of the platform where a group is gathering, sitting on mats on the ground. A lively song service is in session, and the leader is Sanjay Choudry.

Thirty-three-year-old Sanjay often shares his testimony. He grew up in a nonbelieving home. He says he was the black sheep of his family, often getting into mischief. His life went from bad to worse, and soon he became very ill. He suffered much pain and could not walk. It was at the time of his greatest misery that he remembered the little New Testament book that a Christian girl had shared with him. He got it out and read how Jesus Christ healed so many sick people when He was on earth. *I wonder if He would heal me?* Sanjay thought. That night, just before he slept, he prayed, "Lord Jesus Christ, if You are the true and living God, please help me."

That night he had a dream in which he saw a red fireball that grew bigger and bigger until it filled the whole sky. Out of the fire, he heard a voice, which he knew to be the voice of Jesus Christ, say, "Be ready!" From that night the pain left him, and he recovered the use of his legs. He contacted a Christian pastor in the area and was baptized after studying the Christian message more thoroughly. Immediately he began to witness. Since there was no place to meet, he got permission to use the railway station platform.

Each Sabbath Sanjay told the people about Christ and invited them to bring the sick for prayer. Often they prayed for the sick right there on the railway platform, and God worked miracles. One of the men who swept the station platform often stopped to listen to the testimonies and singing and prayers. Then he got sick and became paralyzed. He begged his relatives to carry him on Sabbath to the station platform for prayer. The group surrounded him, and the pastor prayed for him. As soon as the prayer was finished, the sweeper stood to his feet and took a few steps!

Tears streamed down his face as he shouted loudly, "Jesus Christ has healed me! It is a miracle! I can walk again! Praise to Jesus Christ!"

Sanjay, a government employee, plans to resign his secure position and give his life to testifying to God's love and goodness.

THE STRANGER WHO CAME TO TOWN

As Pastor Baka visited the villages in his new district in a remote area of southeastern India, he was met with curiosity, but with little interest in religion.

"We have no place for your God here," one man told him. But one villager, Samuel, was a Christian who had prayed for five years that God would send a pastor. Together the two men held meetings to which 200 people came, and thirty-five requested baptism.

On the day of the baptism, the entire village gathered at the lake to watch. Samuel and his family were baptized first, followed by a young woman.

When the pastor raised the woman from the water, she suddenly cried out in alarm, "My wedding ring is gone! If I go home without it, my husband will beat me!"

"Our God can do anything," Pastor Baka assured her. "If it is His will, He will show us where your ring is."

When he finished baptizing the new believers, Pastor Baka joined them on the shore and asked them to form a circle for prayer. He prayed that God would reveal His power and glory by showing them where the woman's ring was.

The pastor told two young boys to go into the water and stand on the spot where he had baptized the new believers. "Reach into the water and bring up a fistful of sand," he said.

The boys did as they were told, but they found no ring. "Reach in again and bring up more sand," the pastor said.

The villagers watched as the boys searched the lake bottom handful by handful. Could the God of the Christians find a small ring in the sandy bottom of the lake? The crowd pressed closer. Suddenly one of the boys shouted, "I found it!" He held up the woman's ring.

The happy woman cried, "My God, Jesus Christ! You are great!" The new believers praised and thanked God for showing the villagers that He is truly the one, all-powerful God.

The amazed villagers returned to their homes talking about the miracle of the missing ring. Following this dramatic answer to prayer, the entire village wanted to know more about this new God who had come to live in their village.

THE ROAD TO CHRIST

Henny Suwondo's father was a follower of Confucious, and her mother was a Muslim. In 1986 she and her husband became members of a Protestant Christian church. As she became acquainted with various other Christian churches, she decided there was one that she could never join—the Seventh-day Adventist Church. Its teaching about unclean foods repelled her. Her decision was strengthened as she saw nearby Adventist neighbors who lacked many Christian graces.

In 2000 Henny began to diligently study the Bible to deepen her understanding of the Scriptures. At this same time an Adventist woman, Vera Kuswandi, invited her to attend a Sabbath service. The Adventist pastor visited Henny that week. On his second visit she said, "Pastor, you need not return anymore. I will never become an Adventist."

Because of her friendship with Vera, Henny agreed in March to study the Bible with Vera and her husband and their pastor. However, she also invited the pastor and elders from her Protestant church. It was an interesting evening. As the study progressed, Henny clearly saw the Bible position for the topics as they were presented. She continued to invite the Adventist team to her home. She accepted all the messages—with one exception. "I will not stop drinking tea. You have no scripture for forbidding tea."

For one week Henny prepared her daily tea stronger than usual. To her horror she discovered blood in her stool. She prayed, "Please help me, God. I will stop drinking tea." Her prayer was answered without any medical help being needed.

With all her questions answered, Henny was baptized in April. Her testimony is that it was the close friendship of Vera that attracted her to the Bible studies. She was impressed with the strong interest of the group in Bible study. Even during storms, the attendance held. In gratitude to God for her new life in Jesus, she invited all her friends to come to her home. She wanted to express the same love to her neighbors that Vera had shown her.

One day her former pastor paid a visit. "I have failed to bring my mother to Jesus," he told Henny. "Please try to reach her. I would be happy to have her join any Christian church." Henny accepted the challenge. That pastor's mother now worships every Sabbath with Henny.

Henny continues to invite interested persons to her home for an evening of fellowship. This leads to Bible studies. Henny thanks God that in less than two years she has seen more than fifty persons accept the Lord Jesus and be baptized from her Monday evening Bible class. She has another twenty persons preparing for baptism.

As soon as one class has been baptized, she begins another.

A LIGHT TO MY PATH

Bahasa was a deeply spiritual eighteen-year-old Muslim youth living in the western portion of Indonesia. He had memorized large portions of the Qur'an and was careful to answer the call to prayer five times a day.

Bahasa dreamed of having a life filled with success in the business world. A nearby Christian college offered a strong course in business administration. Also, his father heard that the school had foreigners—native English speakers—teaching English. He felt that a knowledge of English was essential for success in the business world, so he enrolled Bahasa in the college.

On the very first day of school the boy found himself attending one of the required religion courses. About halfway through the class the professor asked a question, "Is there anyone here who does not own a Bible?" Bahasa raised his hand. In a rather abrupt manner the teacher pointed his finger at the youth and said, "Do not return to this class without a Bible."

Bahasa was deeply hurt by this embarrassment. The teacher surely knew that he was a Muslim. But, very reluctantly, he went to the college bookstore and purchased a Bible. Filled with still more reluctance and a considerable amount of fear, Bahasa read the assigned portions of Scripture.

But as the weeks passed, something happened. Bahasa began to notice that the Bible contained many of the same stories as did the Qur'an. He was surprised to see that it contained similar stories about Moses, Abraham, and the holy prophets. However, the Bible was better organized. He noticed that it started with the creation of the world and humankind, then moved to the fall into sin. He began to see the amazing love of God in providing salvation for sinners. He thrilled to see that the Bible story ended with a description of heaven.

But the part of the Bible that touched Bahasa's heart the most was the presentation of a Savior. This he found missing in the Qur'an. According to the Qur'an, salvation rests solely upon one's ability to totally submit to God in the strictest obedience. A person is really his or her own savior. For the first time in his life a new thought dawned on Bahasa: *Could it be that the Christian Bible is inspired by God?* It wasn't long before Bahasa felt that he should become a Christian.

"As I look back on this experience," Bahasa testifies, "I am convinced that the Holy Spirit was guiding in my life."

In 1995 Bahasa attended the funeral of the professor who forced him to secure a Bible. By the coffin Bahasa prayed, "Thank You, Lord, for this man who helped me find my way to Your holy Book." Bahasa looks forward to the day when he will meet his teacher in heaven.

A LAY MISSIONARY FOR CHRIST

Fredoy Wondal owns a bakery business in Manado, a city in East Indonesia. For ten years he served as an elder in the Ranotana church. The congregation deeply appreciated his spiritual leadership and his soul-winning activities.

In the summer of 1995 the church board offered to give Fredoy an opportunity to become a full-time soul winner. The board offered him a stipend if he would give all his time to soul winning. Marie, his wife, agreed to manage the bakery so Fredoy would be free to accept the offer. Fredoy's work would be evaluated every three months by the church board.

Fredoy went to work. As he visited every home in his immediate community, he prayed that the Lord would help him find persons interested in Bible study. Soon he was giving Bible studies every day of the week.

When a major evangelistic meeting was planned for Manado, the organizers gave Fredoy a modest budget so he could conduct a small-group meeting as part of the ground work. Every week the Lord blessed Fredoy with converts to Christ.

Fredoy conducted five small-group meetings prior to the major evangelistic meeting. His enthusiasm for the Bible and his energetic preaching touched the hearts of his listeners. He planned his public meetings so that they would end as the guest evangelist began his harvest meeting. Fredoy arranged transportation to bring his little flock to attend the larger meeting. His Bible lessons were reinforced in the second meeting, and many of his group took their stand for Jesus when the calls for decision were made.

Fredoy continues to work diligently for the Lord. He spends many hours in personal work, often going from door-to-door in Manado looking for persons who will open their homes for Bible study. Once he finds a home, the owner will often invite his neighbors and friends to attend. During the small-group meetings, the participants develop camaraderie and close spiritual fellowship. They pray together, supporting one another through personal difficulties while they study the Bible with Fredoy. Within weeks many are ready to take the step of baptism. In other homes, he conducts a Bible study just for the immediate family.

Fredoy fills every available hour with these Bible studies. The Ranotana church plans to continue supporting Fredoy as its own full-time missionary for the Lord.

A SOUL-WINNING TEAM

Ellen and John Lanes are a couple with a mission. They use their individual skills and the gifts of hospitality to win others for Christ in the large city of Manado, on the East Indonesian island of Sulawesi (Celebes).

John is a bus driver in Manado. As he guides his bus along his appointed route, he looks for ways to give his passengers more than just a safe ride to their destination. He tries to guide them to a better life. He serves many of the same customers several times a week, and John strikes up conversations, seeking to develop a friendship with them.

When a smoker boards his bus, John looks for ways to help the person see the danger of the habit. He shares with his clients the latest scientific information regarding the health hazards of tobacco or alcohol. As he tries to help those who have a problem with a harmful habit, he often can share his faith. And if a person expresses an interest in spiritual things, John invites him or her to attend one of his Bible classes.

Ellen Lanes is a seamstress. When a woman comes to her with sewing needs, Ellen sees more than a customer; she sees a friend. Through repeated contacts with her customers, Ellen nurtures their friendship and invites them to attend one of her Bible study groups.

The Lord has given John and Ellen Lanes the gifts of hospitality and teaching. Every month they bring converts to the Lord. In the first four years after John and Ellen began their outreach activities, they brought seventy-five souls to Christ.

John and Ellen exemplify the spirit of East Indonesia where Christians are organized into small teams and where lay members are eager to reach out to their friends and neighbors with the good news of Jesus and the salvation that He offers to all. John and Ellen Lanes are just two of the many Christian Indonesians who have accepted God's commission to love their neighbors as themselves.

KINDNESS REPAID

Dr. Rudyanto is a Christian physician and businessman living in Solo, Indonesia. One morning he awoke to the sounds of angry shouting and stones bouncing off the metal doors of his furniture shop, which adjoins his home. From his window, he could see flames devouring a business across the street.

For some time tensions between the ethnic Chinese population and Muslims had been spreading throughout Indonesia. Now the animosity had erupted into open violence with mobs rioting in the streets, destroying property and even life.

The police were powerless to stop the rampaging rioters. The Rudyanto family gathered to ask for God's protection.

The hail of stones increased. Then the doctor heard someone trying to break in through the heavy, iron doors that protected the building. If the rioters succeeded, the doctor's family would be in serious danger.

Suddenly, another group of voices began shouting in front of the building. Dr. Rudyanto watched amazed as some twenty-five Muslim men pushed their way through the mob and refused to let the rioters destroy the building. Dr. Rudyanto recognized the men; they lived in a small settlement of poor families nearby. He had treated many of their medical needs, often without any charge if they could not pay. Sometimes he had given them medicine from his pharmacy, and on occasion he had even taken them food when he knew a family to be in financial distress.

Now these neighbors stood between the rioters and the doctor's family, shouting, "Please leave! The doctor is a good man; he is our friend. Do not harm his property!"

After the mob moved on, the Muslim men remained to guard the building as other rioters stormed down the street, stealing and destroying everything. For hours they continued to protect the Christian doctor and his family.

One of their Muslim friends urged the Rudyanto family to come to his home, where they would be safer. The family slipped out the rear door and followed the man home. They remained in the home of their friend until the riots ended.

Why did these Muslims risk their lives to protect a Chinese Christian family? "They are our friends," one man answered. "When we are sick or in need, they help us." The doctor and his family thank the Lord that He has helped them to live as representatives of Jesus before their neighbors.

THE MAN WITH A BLACK BOOK

The sun disappeared behind the hills of central Sulawesi, Indonesia, as we hiked up a narrow jungle trail. In the darkness we stumbled over fallen trees, slippery stones, and across logs that bridged rushing streams. The three-hour hike stretched to seven hours before we arrived at the tiny village hidden among jungle spice orchards.

Quickly I fell asleep on my bed of rough boards, with no mattress or blankets, and awoke to the sound of children at play.

The local church leader invited me to his home. As do most of the villagers, the elder lives in a tree house high above the clove orchards. In the days of tribal wars, villagers found safety from enemies by climbing into their tree houses and pulling their ladders up after them.

The elder's wife, with an infant tied to her hip, quickly mounted the thirty-foot bamboo ladder to her house. "Come on in," her husband invited me, ascending the ladder. Slowly, I climbed the rickety steps, certain that my weight would break the slender bamboo steps that led to their two-room house. Gingerly I sat down in the doorway, enjoying the sights and sounds of the village as he told me a story.

Many years before, a woman had dreamed that a man came into the village carrying a black book. The villagers gathered around the stranger as he spoke. "Friends, I have brought with me the Book of the God of heaven. This Book tells us about Jesus, who died for our sins, and about the Sabbath of God."

Years passed. Then one day a pastor hiked over the same trail on which I had walked the day before. He carried a Bible and spoke the same words that the woman had heard in her dream years before.

The woman shouted in joy, "Brothers, this man has a message from God for us!" Today almost everyone in that village is a church member. They have carried the gospel of the black Book to eleven neighboring villages.

Thousands of villages still wait for someone to bring the story of Jesus. Will you help?

PROTECTED FROM FIFTY KILLERS

Imagine a sixty-one-year-old widow riding with a group on an empty logging truck. The semi-trailer has no sides or floor. Joy and her team each cling with one hand to one of the two cross pieces where the logs ordinarily rest. With the other hand they cling to one of the four upright beams. The rough road makes the ride even more dangerous. A single bump might cause them to lose their hold and fall beneath the dual wheels of the truck and be crushed to death.

Once each year, Joy and her team make a trip to one of the remote villages of Myanmar (formerly Burma) to conduct an evangelistic meeting. In 1995 she was on her way to Nat Mon village. This community is half Christian and half Buddhist. The people earn their living marketing jade and opium. The main thrust of their lives is enriching themselves. Religion takes a second place.

The majority of the people of Nat Mon were not interested in the gospel. However, some of the Buddhists were impressed by the Bible stories and the help that the team offered with their health problems. But another group, which resented the work of Joy and her team, hired fifty men to kill the missionary team. The village became divided. Some demanded death for the evangelists, but others suggested that Joy and her team be driven out of the village instead.

Joy and her team offered earnest prayers for God's protection. They could not think of leaving without giving the message of the gospel. They had come a long and difficult way.

The attendance at their meetings grew. Many were impressed by the spirit of Joy's team. The Buddhists began to rally around the missionaries. By the grace of God the team finished their work without harm.

Joy led another team to Pa Doh village. "This place was so different from Nat Mon. The people were eager to hear about the truth of the gospel," Joy stated.

One of the persons preparing for baptism became ill with a high fever. On the day of the baptism the team told her that she was too sick to make the long trip to the river. She could become chilled. When the team and their baptismal candidates arrived at the river however, the sick girl stepped into the line for baptism. She had followed the group at a distance. "I must be baptized. I want to be ready to meet Jesus," she pleaded. Instead of becoming more ill, her fever left her.

EAGER TO SERVE

The evangelism training seminar in Germany had just ended. As Uwe Wiesenberg, one of the participants, drove home, he was eager to share his faith with someone. But this was Germany, where people's materialistic focus makes witnessing for Christ difficult. As Uwe drove, he asked God to help him find someone who needed to know Him.

He stopped to visit his Uncle Paul, a hospital nurse who also had attended the seminar. As Uwe stood in the hospital foyer, an old man walked up and began talking to him. He told Uwe that he had decided to end his life.

Uwe guided the man to a bench and listened as he unburdened his heart, telling a story of heartache and disappointment. Uwe could understand why the man was so deeply depressed.

When the man stopped talking, Uwe shared his faith in God and his confidence in the power of prayer. He shared the story of Jesus and the love of God, which led Jesus to die on the cross.

"God loves you very much," Uwe offered. "He will forgive your sins and fill your heart with joy and peace. He will make you a new man." Then the two men prayed together.

Hope flickered in the man's eyes, and a smile crept across his face. Then he asked, "May I go to church with you?"

As Uwe began to explain that he does not live in Neustadt, his Uncle Paul walked up. Uwe introduced him to the old man and relayed the man's request to go to church. Paul promised to take him the next Sabbath and told him that after church they could go for a walk in the Black Forest where they could commune with God. Paul also arranged with the man to begin Bible studies.

"I've never met such wonderful people in all my life!" the old man smiled. Uwe and Paul gave him a copy of *Steps to Christ*, then the three men prayed.

The old man said, "I wanted to end my life today; now I have been born anew!"

Uwe's enthusiasm bubbled over as he shared how, in just one hour, God had answered his prayer for one soul by bringing this man to him.

"He came in despair, and now he has hope," Uwe said. "I thank God for the power of the Holy Spirit. Souls can be won to Jesus even here in Germany."

A FITTING WAGE

"Bernd, can you do the electrical wiring on my new house?" Heiner asked his brother. Heiner was pleased that his brother, an electrician, agreed. When the job was done, Bernd stopped to see his brother on the way to a Sabbath-evening evangelistic meeting.

Heiner was surprised to find his brother at the door, especially on the Sabbath. "I have come to collect my wages for wiring your house," Bernd said.

"How much do I owe you?" Heiner asked apprehensively, for he was short of cash. "Change your clothes and come with me to the meeting tonight. That will be my fee." Relieved, Heiner agreed and hurried to change his clothes. One meeting in exchange for his brother's work was too good a deal to pass up.

The meeting awakened in Heiner warm memories of his childhood when he had attended the local Adventist church with his mother and brothers. But he had not been to church for twenty years. Heiner returned the next night and every night of the series. Following the meetings, Heiner was baptized. Then the brothers began praying for Heiner's wife, Carola. A year later, in 1982, she was baptized.

Heiner wanted to share his faith with others, but wasn't sure how to start. He placed an ad in the local newspaper, inviting anyone interested in reading the Bible to come to his home. Soon he had a small group meeting each week. After several weeks, three persons were baptized. Heiner and Carola prayed for three new persons to take their places.

In the sixteen years since they began their home Bible meetings, Heiner and Carola have seen fifty persons join the family of God. These individuals came because they saw the newspaper ad or were invited by friends.

Heiner and Carola have started a new church in a neighboring town. One family who came was from Kenya. This family was baptized and eventually returned to Kenya and started a new church there.

Heiner and Carola are working with four small groups. The work has grown so large that Heiner now trains other church members to lead out in some of the groups. Carola started a very successful women's ministry group in their church. "Our greatest joy comes from seeing what God can do to bring people to a new life," Heiner and Carola say. They should know; they themselves are the fruits of witnessing by Heiner's brother.

KILL THE OLD MAN!

Jardslaw Wajik, a popular rock-band musician in Poland, had everything he wanted. Everything but peace. He had grown up attending church, but his life had become a tangled nightmare of tobacco, drugs, alcohol, and sinful living. He knew that his lifestyle was killing him. Depression set in, and one night he sat on a street curb and cried.

He was admitted to a mental hospital, and slowly his life began to change. Following his release, he married a former Christian who helped him recover his health. His music career soared, and his records reached the top of the charts. But, in spite of success and financial security, Wajik still felt lonely.

When one of his band members announced that he intended to stop smoking, Wajik, who smoked seventy cigarettes a day, replied, "If you are still clean in two weeks, I will stop smoking too." Two weeks later Wajik knew he must keep that promise. He asked God to take away his hunger for liquor and tobacco. God came close to him and answered his prayer.

Then one day Wajik's wife announced that she had been rebaptized. She wanted a new life for herself and their daughter. Wajik did not object. One day he picked up a Bible, and in his own words, "The Lord opened it to Exodus 20." He read the Sabbath commandment and realized that the church of his childhood was not following all the commandments. He stopped performing in rock concerts on Sabbath.

He attended evangelistic meetings, but did not take a stand for God. Several months later at a youth camp meeting, Wajik felt the Holy Spirit touch his heart. He gave his heart totally to God. At his baptism Wajik testified, "My old life was buried in the water, and Jesus has given me a new life. I am still a sinner, but I have a wonderful Friend, Jesus Christ."

God impressed him that he needed to use his influence and popularity to help others. He dropped out of his band and set his heart on three objectives. He wanted to have a relationship with God, a God-honoring family, and to be involved in some exemplary type of work. He had no idea how hard that would be.

Wajik began writing songs for a new musical group. He wants to show people the way out of sin, the way to joy and hope. He prays that the thousands who purchased his earlier albums will purchase the new one, and find in it the joy that Wajik has found in his new life in Christ.

MARIA'S CELEBRATION OF JOY

When Maria Brozozek retired from her work as a tailor in Poland, she had a burden to help people in her hometown. Her life took a new direction when she learned about a poor family that was not able to pay the rent for their apartment. The owner was about to evict them. Maria asked people in the community to donate used items to be sold and the funds given to this family so they could remain in their apartment.

Her efforts were a success, and Maria began looking for others she could help. She developed a plan to designate a special day for what she called a Celebration of Joy. Then she organized activities that were open to the community. Children prepared a play based on a Bible story; the community was invited to bring used items for an auction following the play. The funds raised were set aside to help the poor.

On one occasion Maria made arrangements for an art exhibition in the city's castle. One of the city's artists provided his art collection for sale. On another occasion actors performed for a benefit show. The proceeds of these events were given to a fund to help the poor.

Maria's program has done a lot to change the attitude of the city's residents toward her church. The local priest has given his blessing for his congregation to support the Celebration of Joy. He even invited the members of Maria's church to present a musical concert in his church to raise funds for the poor.

When people ask Maria why she does this, she tells them how God's love changed her life and that she wants to help change others' lives as well. Television and radio stations have featured Maria's mission, and the newspaper has begun a column listing places where people in need can go for help. Clothing is collected to be given to needy children, and poor children are taken on special field trips.

Many people in Maria's city want to know more about Christianity as a result of Maria's work. Maria is studying the Bible with ten people who might never have become interested had it not been for her Celebration of Joy.

THERE IS A GOD

It was bad news. Mr. Vasele Lupu had developed prostate cancer. His doctor told him that there must be surgery, but that it might be too late to save his life. After the surgery, the elderly man was very ill. During a visit with his son he said, "I may not live. I am very ill." After his son left, the father prayed, "Dear Father, I place myself in Your hands, to live or die, as You will."

His son, Benone, was attending a seminary several miles away and was not able to visit the hospital every day. Two days later, when the son returned, he was surprised to find his father walking down the steps, preparing to go home.

The father told this story, "I don't know if I was dreaming or not, but there was a very bright light at the foot of my bed. Then, I saw a man in the light. He told me that I would live and that there was more work for me to do for God." Mr. Lupu's roommate had not seen the bright light or heard the voice of the man. But as he saw the new strength that came to his fellow patient, he became interested in learning about God.

Fully recovered, the elderly man began visiting the notorious prison in Bucharest. During communism he had spent several years there as a prisoner for his Sabbath keeping. Daily, he had been insulted for his faith in God. The atheistic guards had enjoyed ridiculing him for his faith. Most of those guards still worked at the prison. One of them now, again, openly ridiculed Mr. Lupu because of his faith in God. The years had not changed his thinking.

However, as the guard listened to the messages given in the jail, his heart was strangely touched. He pressed close to listen each time Mr. Lupu visited the prison. His ridicule ended. Now he asked for personal Bible studies. It was a wonderful day when the atheistic communist guard was baptized!

But the guard's wife became very angry with her husband. She felt that he had made a stupid mistake. How could any intelligent person believe that there is a God?

Then one day as he prepared to go to work at the prison, the guard once again attempted to convince his wife of the reality of a deity. In anger and frustration the wife replied, "Do you see this plant? We have had it for many years, and it has never had a blossom. If this plant would bloom, then perhaps I could believe as you do."

Later that same day, as the wife went about her housecleaning, she walked into the room where the barren plant sat. She was amazed to see that it was covered with blossoms! The impossible had taken place. For the first time in her life, faith was awakened in her heart. She studied God's Word and later joined her husband in baptism.

A DRAMATIC CHANGE OF LIFE

Helena was determined to prevent her husband from ever being baptized. She had been very happy when Gregori found work with a Christian employer. The paychecks were a blessing during economic hard times.

But one day his employer invited Gregori to attend a Bible study. Gregori politely turned down the invitation. The boss persisted in encouraging his employee to come. When he heard the testimonies of the other attendees, and fearing that he might lose his job if he continued to decline, Gregori decided he would go just once. It might give him job security.

As he listened to the words of Scripture, he felt his heart strangely touched. He decided he would attend again. Little by little faith awakened in his heart.

When Gregori told Helena that he was considering a decision to be baptized, she became furious. "I don't want you to ever return to that Bible study again," she said.

But Gregori could not stay away and continued to study.

Helena determined to put an end to this new "foolishness." She thought of a plan to turn the employer against her husband. Even his paychecks were not enough to dissipate her anger. She turned off the alarm clock each night after Gregori fell asleep. If she could make him late to work often enough, his friendship with the boss and his interest in the Bible might come to an end.

But the boss understood the problem and forgave Gregori's tardiness.

Then Helena thought of another plan. She would stop cooking. Gregori could starve. If he got hungry enough, he would turn from this foolishness. She was surprised at how patient and kind Gregori had become, even with this new hostility. He still continued to attend the meetings.

Finally, in desperation, she thought of still another plan. She would gather all his clothing, except the work clothes, and burn them. He would have nothing fit to wear to the Bible study or the church services he was now attending.

She gathered all his good clothing. But, as she was about to light the match, a new thought entered her mind. What was it about the Bible and the church that made Gregori willing to take all her persecution so patiently? Helena decided that she would visit once to see what happened at the Bible study. That night she went with Gregori, and she began to understand.

On March 22, 1997, Helena and Gregori were baptized in Radauti, Romania. "I have never been so happy or had such peace in all my life," Helena testified.

APRICOTS FOR SOULS

Alexander Butoy made his escape from communist Romania and, with the Lord's help, eventually settled in Southern California.

When communism collapsed in Romania, Alexander began to pray for ways that he could share his love for Jesus with the people in Mari, the Romanian village of his birth. During a visit in 1992, Alexander took fifty Bibles to Mari. To his surprise he discovered that not one home had a Bible. He made a trip to Bucharest to purchase another 105 copies. Alexander distributed Bibles to every home.

While Alexander was staying in the home of his brother in Mari, two men from a village named Veda came looking for him. "Mr. Butoy, we heard about the work that you are doing here. Please come to our village and share the Bible with our people. Our people would like to have Bibles." Alexander promised that he would try to find a way to help them.

Arriving back in California, he visited two of his cousins whose ancestral home was Veda. "I have provided Bibles for my village. Can you help provide Bibles for your village?" he challenged them. In 1993 Mr. Butoy was accompanied by his cousins when he returned to Romania. They provided a Bible for every family in Veda.

While working from home to home, they met the Orthodox priest. He was very friendly. He expressed appreciation for the fact that every family now had a copy of the Bible. "While I cannot attend your meetings, I will invite my people to attend. It is all right with me if half of the town joins you," was his statement. During mass, he invited his congregation to attend the meetings of the three men from America who brought Bibles to Veda.

In 1994 Alexander decided to take Bibles to six additional villages. When Alexander learned that there were 2,500 families in these villages, he needed help. *The Quiet Hour* and several churches provided 2,500 Bibles.

During one of Alexander's visits to Mari, a man said to him, "Mr. Butoy, we greatly appreciate the Bibles you gave us, but we need help. We are like a cat trying to read a calendar. We don't understand the Scriptures. We need someone to teach us about the Bible."

One day, as Alexander's three apricot trees were in full bloom, he knelt to dedicate one of the trees to the Lord. He would sell all those apricots and provide stipends for laymen to do evangelism in Mari. The Lord blessed that tree with twice the amount of fruit as the other trees. The funds from that tree provided stipends for several lay workers to teach the Bible in Romania. "This has been the most precious experience of my life," is Alexander's testimony.

A DREAM WINS SOULS

Pastor Benone Lupu was preparing to conduct an evangelistic meeting in Sucavita, Romania. He asked his members to support the meeting by inviting their friends. Brother Mircea Gainescu agreed to invite his friends.

However, during the busy activities of the day, he forgot to keep his promise. His pastor asked for his help the second time. But again, with the pressures of family and work, the time slipped by, and the promise was forgotten.

It was Friday night. Brother Gainescu had a dream. He seemed to be looking toward the gate on the street that led to his front door. As he watched, he saw a man. The man was rather short in stature and thin. His hair was curly.

As he watched, the stranger asked whether he could go to church with Brother Gainescu. Mircea headed for the front door to welcome the stranger at the gate when his dream ended, and he woke up.

Then Mircea remembered his broken promises. Shortly after daybreak, he looked out his window toward the front gate. To his great surprise, Brother Gainescu saw a man standing at his gate. The man was short and thin with curly hair. This was the very same man whom he had seen in his dream!

Mircea ran out to the gate and welcomed the man into his home. The stranger voiced a familiar request, "May I go to your church with you? I want to learn how to understand the Bible."

The stranger attended all Pastor Lupu's remaining evangelistic meetings. He thrilled to the message of the gospel. He accepted the presentation of each study with joy. After his baptism, he invited his neighbors to come to his home to study the Bible. Forty persons attended.

Mircea Gainescu rejoiced that the Lord did not let him forget the promise he had made to invite someone to the pastor's evangelistic meeting—and that through that person, he had been able to reach out to many others.

SINGLE MOTHER PLANTS TWO CHURCHES IN SIBERIA

Galina Kazakova's life looked dreary. As a single parent with a daughter to provide for, she found that her work as a nurse's assistant barely paid the bills. Life was hard, but Galina developed a close walk with Jesus. He sustained her through this difficult time.

Galina lives near Irkutsk, on the southern tip of Lake Baikal, in south central Siberia. This huge territory covers five time zones and contains hundreds of towns and cities that have no Sabbath keepers. The region is so vast that some Sabbath-keeping congregations are 600 miles (1,000 kilometers) from the next nearest Adventist congregation.

A thought began to burn in Galina's heart. The city of Cheremhovo and the region surrounding it were almost empty of believers. Someone should share the gospel with the people of this region.

Galina stepped out in faith and took a year's leave from her work. She packed up her few belongings and went to Cheremhovo. She found a place to live and then visited the city manager's office to secure a permit to be a missionary in the city. With her permission document in hand, Galina began visiting schools, orphanages, and factories, offering to give a spiritual message to the students and employees. She sold Christian literature to earn a living as she searched for honest souls who were interested in spiritual matters. She found very few who would agree to study the Bible course she offered.

The work was hard, and her earnings were meager. In a moment of discouragement, she felt as if she were a failure, and she considered returning home. In desperation she poured out her heart to God. "Lord, I want to see a church here in Cheremhovo. I have worked hard, but the way seems impossible. Please, please help me."

The next day Galina received a letter from the Bible correspondence school containing a list of persons who had completed the course. She began visiting the people and giving personal Bible studies. Soon a church was organized in Cheremhovo with fifty-three members.

Galina turned her eyes to the city of Severobaikalsk, another area with no Sabbath keepers. So far, ten persons have been baptized there, and Galina is giving Bible studies to more than fifty others.

During *The Quiet Hour's* training program for volunteer missionaries, Galina committed herself to plant a third church in another city in Siberia. She is joining fifteen other teams in the East Russian Union Mission to plant sixteen new churches in one year.

GOD PROVIDES A WAY

Pastor Michael Melenko did not know what to do. After seventy years of political oppression in Russia, the doors of freedom had swung open, and people swarmed in to hear the message of the gospel. But now that interest appeared to have waned, and in spite of trying many different approaches, it seemed that every door closed to the pastor's efforts to spread the gospel in the city of Perm.

Pastor Melenko did not expect an easy task. His father and grandfather had been pastors during the communist years. He knew the difficulties they had endured during their ministries. Melenko believed that God would open the door for him to share the gospel as well. He and his wife prayed earnestly for a breakthrough.

Michael watched from his seventh-floor apartment window as his three-and-a-half-year-old son, Vadim, played in the courtyard below. A number of *babushkas* (grandmothers) sat nearby, enjoying the sun's warmth in the little courtyard. A few minutes later little Vadim rushed through the door of the apartment. "Please, Mother, may I have my Bible?" he asked, breathless.

"Why do you want your Bible?" she asked. Vadim could not yet read.

"I want to preach to the *babushkas* in the yard," he answered. His mother gave him his little Bible with pictures of his favorite Bible stories, and the little boy raced out the door and back to the courtyard. Vadim's astonished parents watched as the little boy began preaching to the old women who sat in the sun. The women asked Vadim whose son he was. Vadim told them that his father was a pastor, who could tell them even more stories about God if they wished. Several accepted Vadim's offer, and the little boy's witness opened the door of many hearts in Perm.

Several months later, the Melenko family moved to another apartment. Vadim quickly made friends with children in the building. He told them about Jesus and prayed with them. Then he invited them to his apartment to watch videos of Bible stories. Pastor Melenko reports that the children have told their parents about the Bible stories, and this has opened the door for more people to find Christ.

Today a growing group of new believers meets every week in Perm, Russia. When the doors seemed closed, God used a little child to open them and lead people to Jesus.

PIONEERS WORK WITH THE ANGELS

Anatoli Berbeka is a youth from Nizhnekamsk, Russia. His home is Tatarstan, a Muslim republic. During *The Quiet Hour* training seminar, Anatoli gave this testimony, "I have seen that the angels go before us to lead people to accept the holy Bible.

"In my home church in Nizhnekamsk," Anatoli continued, "there is a sister named Svetlana. She comes from a Muslim family. All her life she has suffered from cerebral palsy. I praise the Lord for the way that God has helped her to a new life.

"She is now thirty-one years of age and has experienced many surgeries and other medical services performed with no results. Just a few months ago, while still a Muslim, she decided that she would end all her misery. She began to secure and save some painkilling tablets.

"One day when she was alone at home with the door locked, she poured a glass of water and took out the many pills she had collected. She prepared to take the tablets with the water and end her life.

"As she picked up the glass, she saw a young man with blue eyes coming toward her. In tender tones He spoke to her, 'Svetlana, don't take the pills. God loves you.' She stopped. She had never heard such words about God's love.

"When her mother came home, Svetlana asked her to purchase a Bible. She read it, but could not understand. Then she remembered that she had heard about the Voice of Hope Bible lessons. She enrolled and began to study the Bible."

When Anatoli visited her, he discovered that she had accepted all the Bible teachings and wanted to be baptized. After her baptism, Svetlana began to write poems about the loving care of God. Her cheerful ways have brought great blessings to the new church family that she has joined.

JESUS' METHODS WORK IN EVANGELISM

Andrew Prokolov is a twenty-year-old Global Mission Pioneer from Elabuga, Russia, located in one of the Muslim republics. It was his task to prepare the way for a *Quiet Hour* reaping meeting. Andrew went from apartment to apartment with a religious survey. In one apartment, a Muslim woman filled out his survey. Andrew asked her whether she would be interested in studying the Bible.

The woman became frightened. "I will never betray my faith," she declared. Andrew answered, "Sister, we believe in the same God. You should become acquainted with what is written in the Bible. Many of the stories of the prophets are the same. You will find it easier to study your Qur'an."

The woman accepted the first lesson. When Andrew returned with the second lesson, he found that she had not had time to study. She worked at two jobs in addition to caring for her children and home. From early till late she was very busy.

Andrew came each week, leaving lessons. He often prayed for God to help this Muslim woman with her problems. Andrew visited her for six months. During this time she did not study even one lesson. Then one week Andrew missed his weekly visit and prayer for the woman and her family.

When he returned, she was very happy. "Why did you not visit me last week? I missed your prayer," she said. She continued, "I studied all the lessons during these two weeks. The Bible is a wonderful book. It is easy for me to understand. Do you have other Bible lessons that I can study?" She was determined to continue her study. Andrew gave her a present—a copy of the New Testament.

During another visit the woman asked where she could secure a complete Bible of her own. She purchased one and continued studying "The New Life" Bible course. Upon completing that course, she enrolled in "The Bible Says" course.

Soon, her Muslim friends began to question her, "Why are you leaving your faith? It is dangerous to read the Bible." All this opposition has not stopped her. She has discovered that all people of all nations are equal before God. She also has discovered the amazing love of God that provided a Savior for her.

When she learned that Andrew was a Sabbath keeper she said, "Your church is my church also." Even though she is not baptized, she has begun to pay tithe. As a Muslim, she was careful to return the 2.5 percent that is required in Islam. She is delighted to increase the amount because of her Bible study.

A MUSLIM WITNESS

"If you speak any more about Jesus and the Bible, you will be fired." These harsh words were spoken to Rosa Faracova, a newly baptized Russian believer. Rosa comes from a Tatar Muslim background. During the seventy years of communist suppression, she and many of her people became either agnostics or nominal believers.

Late in 1995 Rosa discovered a fifty-two-year-old Bible that her mother had hidden in a trunk. During the days of communist opposition, there was a hunger for spiritual things, either Muslim or Christian. Her mother had secretly read the Bible.

Rosa thought the Bible was a prayer book. She wanted to learn how to pray. To her surprise, she found the stories of men and women who faced many problems in life. She thrilled to see how God helped them. She read from the Bible daily.

One day she saw an advertisement for a Bible class and eagerly enrolled. As she studied, she found new peace and hope. A few months later she joined seven others to become the first Christian Sabbath keepers in her city.

Now Rosa had a burden to share this new life with her friends and fellow workers. The entire staff with whom she worked were nominal Muslim believers. She wanted them to see and experience the new life she enjoyed.

Witnessing was hard. Some called her a traitor. Others coldly refused to listen to the Bible message. In spite of her productive work, her atheist boss wanted to hear nothing of any religion on the job. Rosa is a single mother with a seven-year-old son to provide for. Jobs are hard to find. She desperately needed to hold her position as a government tax collector.

"Even though I may lose my job, I must tell others about what Jesus has done for me," she says. "I long for my friends to come to know Jesus as their Friend. Please teach me how to share my faith with my Muslim friends and relatives." A translation is being prepared for Rosa, using the Qur'an and the Bible. These lessons highlight the points of our common faith in Jesus—the Sabbath, the Second Advent, healthful lifestyle, and the judgment, among other things.

Rosa asks her Christian brothers and sisters to pray for her and her plans to keep on sharing Jesus with others.

A GLOBAL MISSION PIONEER COUPLE

Viktor Bechterev, a professor of economics, lost his wife in 1992. From his youth he had been an atheist. In his grief, for the first time in his life, he reached out for help to the church. He turned to the Bible, but found it very distasteful. His grief deepened. He had nowhere to turn for help.

Later that year, a leading Russian scientist gave his testimony on how the Bible had changed his life. Viktor decided to try the Bible again. Day by day as he read, his attitude changed.

In 1993 Viktor noticed an invitation to join a Revelation seminar. He began to attend. During the seminar he met Elevantina Kazak, a widow. As they studied together, their friendship deepened. Together, they made two decisions. They would accept Jesus as their Savior, and they would begin a new life together.

In January 1995, following their marriage, they attended the training seminar conducted by *The Quiet Hour* for Global Mission Pioneers. They wanted to share their new faith. They accepted the challenge to spend one year in an unentered city with the goal of starting a new congregation. In February they arrived at Neftekamsk, an unentered city that is 70 percent Muslim.

At first they met a great deal of resistance. Five times they were asked to vacate their living quarters. Almost everyone resisted their invitation to begin Bible studies. Together they prayed for God to open doors for them.

Viktor visited factories, schools, nursing homes, and kindergartens. He offered to present lectures. Before long, he and Elevantina had reached out to more than 900 persons. Slowly, friendships developed. These friendships opened the way for Bible studies to begin.

What joy was theirs when in July they saw eight of their new friends baptized! One of the factories where Viktor has lectured offered the free use of an auditorium for their church services. In September 1996 a *Quiet Hour*/Global Mission team arrived from North America to conduct a harvest meeting. Thirty persons were baptized immediately following the meeting.

Viktor and Elevantina continued studying with 140 interested persons. They nurtured the new believers from week to week. When the new company at Neftekamsk was sufficiently grounded in their new faith, Viktor and Elevantina moved to another unentered city to begin again their outreach for souls who do not know the love of the Lord Jesus.

MIRACLE IN GLASOV

"What are those Americans doing to you?" the middle-aged Russian man asked his wife as she returned from an evangelistic meeting in Glasov, Ukraine. "What drug are they giving you? You have changed so much I hardly recognize you!" The man was suspicious of the dramatic change in his wife's countenance.

Kima had been a manager in a factory and a loyal member of the communist party, with all its privileges. Her high salary provided many comforts her country-men could only dream of.

But the fall of communism brought an abrupt end to Kima's privileged lifestyle. She lost her job and could not find another. She became depressed and lost all hope for the future. She turned to alcohol and tobacco to ease her pain. Each day she seemed to sink lower into a pit of despondency.

Then a young woman invited her to attend some meetings called the "New Way of Life." Kima was an atheist; the Bible and American Christians had no place in her future. In fact, she had plans to end her life, but agreed to go just to see. And God had other plans for her.

"At the meetings, I was amazed. The people were so friendly," Kima testified. "I listened to their prayers, and the Bible touched my heart." Kima purchased some books following the meeting. As she read one book about Jesus, she checked every reference in the Bible she had received. "I felt strangely warmed as I read. I could not put the books down. I spent eight hours in study."

Now Kima is a new person. "I love the Bible. I think I have been born all over to a new life," she says. "If these meetings had been delayed one week, I would have been dead. I had lost all interest in living any longer. I had made plans to end my life. Thank you for coming to Glasov."

Kima is attending one of four house churches in Glasov and is preparing for baptism. She has requested materials so she can help her friends conquer alco-holism. "I no longer yearn for a high position and a large salary. I would be happy to be a street sweeper, as long as I can know Jesus and have His joy in my heart."

DINING CAR EVANGELISM

Larissa Holapova grew up in Tashkent, one of the Muslim republics of the former Soviet Union. While attending the seminary in Zaokski, Russia, she participated in an evangelistic meeting. As she saw some of her interested friends baptized, she thrilled to the thought of giving her life in the service of God.

During a vacation period she took a three-day train trip to visit her mother in Tashkent. As she planned for the three days and nights on the train, a strange thought came to her. *I wonder, could I preach the gospel during the long train trip?* she asked herself.

Larissa made this possibility the subject of earnest prayer. Preaching on a train would be a great challenge. The majority of the passengers would be Muslims. When her friends heard about her plan, some called her crazy.

As Larissa prepared for her trip, she loaded her suitcases with Bibles and literature. She would share these books with those who would listen to her message.

After boarding the train, she went to the head conductor. Larissa asked if she could rent the dining car between meals. When he learned that she planned to teach the similarities between the Bible and the Qur'an, he refused to let her use the car.

As she walked through the dining car, passengers noticed that Larissa was carrying a Bible. "What is that book you are carrying?" someone asked. "Please tell us about the Bible," a man in a railroad uniform asked.

"The head conductor would not let me rent this car to teach the Bible and the Qur'an," she answered.

"I am the director of this dining hall. You may speak here when no meals are being served," replied the man in the uniform.

With a prayer in her heart Larissa began to speak. The car soon filled with Muslims. They were surprised to learn that the Bible taught about worshiping one God who created all things, the sin of idolatry, the importance of the law of God, and the need for a deeper spiritual life as one prepares for the judgment. There are so many similarities between the Qur'an and the Bible.

When Larissa settled in her car, a crowd soon gathered at the door. She spent hours talking with the interested persons.

Upon the completion of her studies Larissa plans to return to Tashkent to share the truths that have brought her hope and assurance.

GOD HONORS A MAN OF FAITH

"We must build a church in the Santa Barbara region of Quito," Vicente Cumbe said to his wife, Laura. Vicente had visited several lovely churches in North America with rooms for children's classes, and he began to dream of having such a church for Santa Barbara. He began searching for a piece of land. After several refusals on the part of landowners, he became discouraged. One day he became angry with God because there was no answer to his prayers. At 2 A.M. one morning he prayed, "Lord, if You want a church in this part of the city, You will need to bring someone to me. I'm not going to look for land any longer." Three days later, a stranger offered Vicente an excellent piece of land. The price was good, and there was enough room for a large church with rooms for the children's classes and even an elementary school.

The little group of believers, led by Vicente, was meeting in a garage at that time. When the other church members heard of Vicente's plan to build a church that would house 450 members with several children's rooms and land for a school, they tried to discourage their friend, "We will never have that many believers in this place. And we do not have the funds for such a large project," they told him.

But Vicente could not drop his dream for Santa Barbara. "I know my God is able to help us, even if we do not have sufficient funds," was his reply.

The income from his little vegetarian restaurant and bakery business was small. "Lord," Vicente prayed, "help Laura and me to find a new product to sell. I will give a second tithe for the new church."

They began selling fresh fruit juice. The first few days' gross sales reached only 30,000 *sucres* (about US$8.00) per day. Vicente and Laura continued to pray, "Lord, help us to sell more, and we will give 20 percent above our tithe." The Lord blessed, and the new juice business grew. Soon the Cumbes were grossing $400 per day and were giving 40 percent in addition to their tithe!

Early in 1997 a group from the eastern United States went to Ecuador to help construct the main shell of the new church. It was with tears in their eyes and joy in their hearts that the Cumbes and the little company saw their new church rise on its foundation.

The little company in Santa Barbara is growing. They have avoided debt. Week by week, as the funds have come in, construction has gone forward. During July 1997, windows were installed, the roof was put on, and Santa Barbara sponsored its first evangelistic meeting. As a result, the little company grew to seventy members. Vicente believes that the new church will one day be too small for the members who will come to the church and that someday an elementary school will be added to the lot that the Lord provided.

"HELP ME, I'M DYING!"

Gustavo Guzman, one of a team of volunteers from Battle Creek, Michigan, was about to step onto the platform to give his health talk during an evangelistic meeting in Esmeraldas, Ecuador, when Jesus Morales came to him with a request, "The doctor said there is no hope for me. I am dying. Please tell me how to be ready to die."

Mr. Morales has an enlarged heart. He went to the hospital in great pain, hoping to find some relief. The cardiologist was not present because it was after office hours. The intern on duty was not able to help.

In desperation this sick man decided that he must talk with a pastor. He knew he was not ready to die. He thought of a saintly woman with whom he worked. He knew that her church was in a certain section of the city. He left the hospital and began to walk, looking for the church. But the churches he found were all closed since it was evening.

So it was with great joy that he finally saw lights in a church and a group of people walking toward the open doorway. An evangelistic team from the United States was conducting a meeting. Gus Guzman, a nurse from Battle Creek, was the first person whom Jesus met.

After Gus finished his health presentation, he talked further with Jesus. "Please help me," pleaded the sick man. "The doctors tell me that I cannot live. I may even die tonight. I want to be ready to die."

As Jesus heard the story of the Savior and His love, a great peace came over him. He felt new strength. Daily, thereafter, he attended the evangelistic meetings. He pleaded with Gus to spend time with him. "I have never met a man more hungry for the Word of God," stated Gus. "We spent two hours each day studying the Bible."

Jesus Morales made the decision to be baptized. The peace of God filled his heart. The fear of death has been removed. And Gus has experienced the greatest joy in his life—knowing that God used him to bring Jesus Morales to the Lord.

THE FALSE PROPHET

Marco Martinez often preached in his church in Santa Lucia, Honduras. The congregation appreciated his efforts until he began quoting from a book that his wife, Norma, had brought home. The book, *The Great Controversy*, had a strong impact on Martinez's sermons. But some of the church members began questioning his theology, and some even called him a false prophet.

One thing bothered Norma. Their church taught that women should not hold leadership roles or take an active part in the local congregation. So when she accepted an invitation to visit the little Adventist congregation in town, she was attracted by the members' freedom to use their spiritual gifts. She began attending this church regularly.

Norma rejoiced in the love, fellowship, and opportunities to serve in her new church. And her husband enjoyed reading the books she brought home. As he read *Steps to Christ,* he was touched by the love of Jesus. He longed to learn more about the Bible.

When the leaders of their home church realized that Norma was attending the Adventist church, they voted to punish Martinez for allowing his wife to leave their church. He was ostracized, and members avoided him. Martinez missed the close fellowship he had once enjoyed in his church.

About this time Norma's church sponsored evangelistic meetings. Martinez attended with his wife and decided to join Norma in her new church. Not one to sit in the pew for long, Martinez circulated through the audience during the altar call one evening, encouraging others to take their stand for Christ and join the church with him.

After his baptism, Martinez organized a Bible study group in his home. In his free time he hikes over the steep mountain trails looking for interested persons with whom he can share his faith. Martinez takes his turn preaching, for his new church shares its pastor with several other congregations. His sermons are similar to those he preached in his former church, but now when he quotes from his favorite books, he is no longer called a false prophet.

YEARS OF PRAYERS

Julia Rodrigues looked up from the pile of laundry she was washing in the pond near Santa Lucia, Honduras. Tina Swazo had placed a copy of *Signs of the Times* beside her and indicated it was for her. Julia thanked Tina for the magazine, adding, "I cannot read, but I will ask my husband to read it to me." Tina promised to visit her.

When Julia brought the magazine home, her husband recognized it from the days when he had worked at a Christian hospital. "This is a good magazine" he told his wife. "Yes, I will read it to you."

Tina visited Julia and her husband and invited them to study the Bible. She took extra time to read each lesson to Julia. When evangelistic meetings were held in Santa Lucia, Julia, her husband, and their daughter took their stand and were baptized. They became the only Sabbath keepers in the village.

Julia memorized the Bible lessons and began visiting door-to-door searching for people interested in studying. Soon three of her neighbors were baptized. Encouraged, Julia continued to work and pray for the people in Santa Lucia.

Years passed, and Julia remained the pillar that held the little church group together. She faithfully prayed that God would bring the thirty friends with whom she studied to a decision for baptism. Then, some twenty years after her own baptism, another evangelistic series was held in Santa Lucia. All thirty of Julia's Bible students were baptized! As 1999 drew to a close, believers from North America flew to Honduras to build a chapel for the believers in Santa Lucia. "This is more than I ever dreamed of asking for in my prayers," Julia said, thrilled. "We now have the finest church in Santa Lucia."

Julia still hikes up and down the steep mountain trails, praying and searching for others who need to hear God's final call. She invites people to follow along in their Bibles as she quotes texts from memory and guides them through the truths that she loves.

Thus through her persistent prayers and hard work, Julia's church in Santa Lucia, Honduras, continues to grow.

GOD'S POLICE SQUAD

General Ramiro Rojas is the commander of one of the most unusual police forces in the world. He leads the 130,000 officers of the national police force in Peru.

Several years ago an event took place that changed the course of Rojas's life and eventually touched the lives of millions in Peru. An Adventist police officer, a close friend of Rojas, was a faithful Christian. When the Adventist officer died in an accident, his widow told Rojas, "If my husband were alive today, he would want you to take his place as an Adventist police officer in this city."

"I will do it," Rojas promised. And he did.

Rojas's new beliefs brought changes to his command. His troops became known for their honesty, refusal to take bribes, and high morale. The commander of the police at the time was dealing with serious ethical problems in the police force. He noticed the differences in Rojas's unit and asked his secret for raising the standard among those under his command.

Rojas answered, "Love for Jesus is changing my officers. They are learning to honor God." Rojas's squad became a model for the entire police force. Eventually, Ramiro Rojas became the commander of the entire Peruvian police force. His influence and leadership touch every police officer and virtually every citizen of the country.

When we visited Rojas in his office, he invited us to kneel for prayer. I was impressed as he poured out his heart to God.

A few minutes later his staff entered, and the general led them in a rousing gospel song, a Bible reading, and a short talk. After several staff members prayed, the group sang another lively song. After they returned to their duties, General Rojas said, "We begin each day with God."

Rojas introduced us to Samuel Cueva, a recent graduate of Andrews University whose job is to share the ethical principles of the Bible with the police force of Peru. Rojas has formed small groups in every police unit to minister to the officers' spiritual needs. More than 500 officers have accepted Christ as their Savior and have been baptized. No pressure is placed on these officers to make a decision for Christ. They simply accept the spirit of prayer and Bible study put into place by Rojas and his team. The Holy Spirit does the rest.

General Rojas said, "God has changed the spirit of my officers!"

A MISSIONARY MOTORCYCLE OFFICER

Captain Gregorio Montoya, leader of the 207-officer motorcycle unit in Lima, Peru, was concerned. His wife worked in the office of General Ramiro Rojas, the Christian commander-in-chief of the 130,000 police force of the nation.

Mrs. Montoya was becoming interested in the general's church. She had joined one of the hundreds of small groups that General Rojas had started. She enjoyed the singing, fellowship, Bible reading, and prayer time. One day Captain Montoya told his wife, "This interest in religion must stop. You must make a decision. It is either me or that small group."

In spite of his threats, she not only continued attending the small group, she began to attend church. She would rise early Sabbath mornings while her husband was still asleep, quietly slip out of her home, and put on her shoes while on the porch. One Sabbath, the captain got up and followed her to church. He was determined to find out what was so compelling about church.

That was a few years ago. Captain Montoya never stopped attending services with his wife. He was baptized in 1996.

Now Captain Montoya conducts devotions with his motorcycle officers. Nearly twenty-four officers, six of whom are women, stand at attention during the changing of shifts, when a short devotional is presented. This is followed by the enthusiastic singing of a gospel hymn. After closing prayer, the group receives the orders for the day.

Captain Montoya testifies, "I want my officers to follow the righteous principles of the Word of God. None of us is paid a high salary. There is always a great temptation to accept bribes. I tell my team, 'If you take so much as one *solé,* you will lose your job and your soul. It is not worth it.' "

Six of Captain Montoya's officers were baptized in the two years following his baptism. Many others are continuing to study the Bible. In his off-duty hours Captain Montoya conducts small Bible study groups for his neighbors and friends.

With a sense of pride and determination Captain Montoya testifies, "With God's help, and as our police force discovers Bible principles, Peru will have the best police force in the world."

ENLARGE THE VISION

Linda de Romanette is a medical doctor with a burden for evangelism. She was looking for a powerful way to uplift the Lord Jesus before large groups of people. She decided on radio. She and her family developed a station in Columbia, South Carolina. The station's call letters, WBAJ, stand for "We Broadcast About Jesus."

The station is unlike most religious radio stations, for it broadcasts no music or news, just sermons, Bible studies, mission reports, and a few public service programs. Each day, listeners hear sermons centered on the Word of God, including sermons on the Sabbath and the soon coming of Jesus. "But," some may ask, "does anyone listen?" Since it first began broadcasting in September 1999, the station has received such a positive response that a second station is being planned.

In the first fifteen months of broadcasting fourteen persons were baptized as a direct result of the radio station, and others are preparing for baptism. Letters and calls from listeners indicate that many more are attending churches in the listening area, which includes South Carolina and Georgia.

One woman named Karen discovered WBAJ while she was driving in her car. She was so excited about hearing the gospel preached that she listened for hours. Because she had no radio in her home, she sat in her car to hear the gospel presentations. And because it was cold outside, she kept the car running to stay warm, using a great deal of gas. Finally, her husband bought her a radio so she could come into the house to listen to the radio! Karen has since been baptized.

Callers report that they like the speakers, most of whom they have never heard preach before. Hundreds have signed up for Bible studies through sponsoring programs such as *The Voice of Prophecy, The Quiet Hour,* and *Amazing Facts.* And a Baptist minister and his wife have offered to do volunteer work for the station.

Although operating a radio station is a heavy financial burden, Dr. de Romanette believes that the Lord will help her to meet the monthly expense. In fact, she is so delighted by the outreach that WBAJ is having that she is planning to sponsor a second radio station. She is finding that ministering to people's souls has been more satisfying for her than ministering to their physical needs. She looks forward to meeting many people in heaven who will trace their relationship to Jesus back to WBAJ.

"DON'T LET OUR CHURCH CLOSE!"

"Dear Lord, help us keep our church open," Cheryl Hodge and Marie Pesak of Rochester, Indiana, prayed. Their little church was the only Sabbath-keeping church in the county. During World War II it had been home to sixty members, but people had moved away over the years or slipped away until only two members remained. But the women were determined to do all they could to keep their church alive.

Then one Sabbath morning Patrick Noonan walked into the church. "I want to be baptized," he announced. The surprised women listened to his story of how family problems had driven him to find the Lord.

"Praise God!" Marie and Cheryl said. "You can be our elder!" The church had just increased its membership by 50 percent, to three active members!

For five years Patrick met with the two women to pray, "Lord, help us keep the light of truth shining in this county." Then in 1993, another member joined the church; Cheryl was married!

Besides their constant and earnest prayers, the four church members worked hard to draw interests from the neighborhood. They held a prophecy seminar that resulted in six new members—more than 100 percent growth! Encouraged, they planned another seminar that helped bring in four additional members.

Other Adventists saw the church members' zeal and transferred their memberships to the Rochester church. Then Pastor David de Pinto was assigned to the little congregation. Impressed by the group's dedication to evangelism, the pastor and his wife settled in, determined to stay and help the church grow.

More seminars, more outreach, and lots more prayer have brought other new members to the church. Today some thirty believers worship and fellowship in the Rochester church. "It is sharing the love of Jesus that attracts people," Marie Pesak says with a smile. "The light of God's truth is shining brightly in Rochester, thanks to the Lord's blessing and eight years of praying, 'Lord, help us keep this church open.'"

THE JOYRIDE

Christopher was in and out of trouble on the New Mexico Navajo reservation where he grew up. Eventually he ended up on probation. He decided to enroll in Holbrook Indian School, a Christian institution that serves Native Americans, in order to straighten himself out.

But Christopher again fell in with the wrong crowd. One of the boys got the keys to the school vehicle. One night, after the school watchman left, several boys crept out a window and took a joyride in one of the school's cars. They carefully returned the car to its parking space and slipped back into the dormitory before anyone saw them.

Emboldened by their success, the boys tried it again the next night. They drove to a town thirty minutes away from school and again managed to return the vehicle without being seen.

On the third night, they decided to visit Phoenix, more than three hours away. Although they started out just after midnight, they soon realized that they had to hurry if they were to be back before daybreak. They turned around and started for the school. As the fourteen-year-old driver sped down the highway to avoid being caught with the car, they were instead stopped by a highway patrol officer.

The officer called the boys' parents to pick them up at the local jail, and the school dean picked up the vehicle. Since the boys planned to return the vehicle, the school did not press charges. But three of them were placed on six months' probation. However, Christopher was almost eighteen, and his part in the joyride broke his probation. He was sentenced to spend spring break in a state correctional facility.

Christopher missed the school trip, which he had been looking forward to. But the experience in the correctional facility gave him time to examine his life and see that he was headed in the wrong direction. When he was released from the correctional facility, he returned to the school a different person. He asked for Bible studies and gave his heart to Jesus. Staff and students rejoiced when, as the school year ended, Christopher was baptized.

Christopher plans to graduate from Holbrook and go on to college as the Lord opens the way. "That careless joyride has opened a whole new life for me," he says. "I thank Christian teachers for their love and guidance. Their response to my behavior has shown me what the forgiveness of Christ is all about."

THE CHANGED HEART

"My husband hates the Bible!" the woman wept. "He was angry when he found me reading it. He threw it against the wall, then he tore it up. Finally, he tried to burn it. This is all that I have of my Bible." She held up a few torn pages. "Then yesterday he struck my five-year-old daughter on her head. I don't know what to do."

Mrs. Dauphney listened carefully as the woman poured out her misery. Then she said, "God loves you. And He does answer prayers. May I pray with you now?" After the women prayed, Mrs. Dauphney told her friend about some seminars being held nearby to help families find happiness.

Just then the woman's husband came home. Out of work, he was angry and desperate. He told how a friend had offered to help him secure drugs that he could sell to earn money. Again Mrs. Dauphney listened. Then she said quietly, "God loves you and your family. He wants a better life for you. God is faithful, and His promises in the Bible are true."

The man asked, "Can you help me get a Spanish Bible?"

Mrs. Dauphney tried not to show her surprise and joy. "Yes, I can get a Bible for you," she smiled.

The following day Mrs. Dauphney brought the man a Bible and stayed to study with the couple. She invited them to attend an evangelistic series, and to her joy, they both agreed to come. The couple took turns attending the meetings while one of them remained in their unfinished home to guard the family's meager possessions.

Each morning Mrs. Dauphney joins the two pastors and thirty-four church members to give progress reports, plan their daily visitation, and pray for the nearly 500 people interested in the Bible. Through their efforts more than 1,000 people have come to the evangelistic meetings each night.

As Mrs. Dauphney shared how God changed the heart of an angry husband, her eyes filled with tears of joy. He and his wife are preparing for baptism. God used the talents of a simple woman filled with love to win a family to Himself. He can use you, too, if you are willing to let Him.

HELPING HANDS LEAD TO BIBLE STUDIES

As Garneita Goffar and her husband moved into a condo with 319 neighbors, one thought possessed her, *How can I witness to my new neighbors?* The condo was a busy place. Taxi cabs often stopped to pick up passengers headed for medical offices, the airport, or shopping places. Many of her neighbors had a serious transportation problem. A person without an automobile lives a very inconvenient life in most North American communities.

Then a thought came to Garneita. *Why not offer to help her new neighbors?* She prepared a note for the bulletin board at the entrance to the condo complex. It was right to the point, "Please give me a call if you need a ride to an appointment." The first callers were hesitant. *What was this person up to? Was it safe to ride with a stranger?*

Soon the calls began to come regularly. There were trips to the airport, doctors' offices, and shopping centers. It wasn't long before there were repeat calls for a ride.

One curious neighbor asked the questions that many had undoubtedly entertained, "Why are you doing this? Who are you anyway?" Another asked, "Are you a Christian?" Then, with a big smile, she asked another question, "Would you be willing to study the Bible with me?"

One day a divorced woman moved into an apartment a couple of doors away from the Goffar condo. Garneita understood how challenging moving is when you are all alone. She greeted her new neighbor, "I would like to get acquainted with you. I live a couple of doors away." Then she continued, "May I wash your windows while you are unpacking your things?" The two women spent several hours working together.

A couple of days later the new neighbor commented to Garneita, "You're different. Are you a Christian?" When the "yes" answer came, she continued, "Why don't we start a Bible study and invite others?" Garneita praises the Lord Jesus that He has opened the way for her to reach out to her neighbors.

"It has taken quite a long time and many trips in my car to various places before my neighbors learned to trust me," Garneita reported. Then she requested, "Please pray for the condo Bible studies in Ft. Lauderdale, Florida."

Garneita gave this testimony during a seminar on evangelism at the Florida camp meeting. Immediately upon returning home, she began two new Bible studies with several neighbors.

GOD FILLS AN EMPTY CUP

"Just like the Samaritan woman who ran back to her village to tell her friends about Jesus," Mrs. Chung says, "I cannot stop sharing Jesus."

Mrs. Chung was searching for God's will in her life. She earnestly prayed that God would lead her to the right church. There were so many denominations! One day she prayed for three hours, "Guide me to the truth, God." Her prayer was interrupted by a knock at the door. When she opened the door, she found several people standing there who had come to invite her to church.

Mrs. Chung attended their church, but she hesitated to join. For months she had felt no peace; her life seemed empty and meaningless. One night, feeling she had reached a new low point, she prayed earnestly and confessed her sins. She promised to follow the Lord wherever He led. At dawn she went to her friends' church to pray. Soon she found assurance that God had accepted her. She began attending the church regularly and was baptized in May 1993.

Her one goal became to share Jesus with others.

When she learned that her cousin's husband was ill with cancer, she visited him. She prayed for him, and God answered her prayers.

She started giving Bible studies to a neighbor couple. What a joy she felt when these friends were baptized!

But her greatest burdens were for her husband and her mother. Her husband never attended church and had some unhealthful habits. She prayed for him, and God answered her prayers. Her husband is now a faithful Christian.

Her mother resisted Mrs. Chung's invitations to study the Bible. Finally she joined a Revelation seminar, but she seemed cold and distant. Mrs. Chung begged God to touch her heart. Her joy knew no bounds when her mother accepted God's call and was baptized last year—along with two of her friends.

Today, her mother is an active soul winner. Because her husband owns several businesses, she has friends among the affluent people in her community. She conducts several Bible studies, cooking classes in her home, and regular Revelation seminars. Her motto is "to work for souls until Jesus comes." She has won seventeen persons to the Lord in the first year since her baptism!

FRIENDSHIP PLANTS A NEW COMPANY

When Melvin Steinke needed to move closer to his work in the logging industry, he and Eileen purchased a home in Rock Creek, British Columbia, Canada. With no church or fellow worshipers nearby, they set out to make friends.

Eileen did not look for employment. Homemaking gave her some freedom to get acquainted with neighborhood women. "As we reached out to people, they soon began inviting us to their clubs," Eileen said. In a short time Eileen was attending two women's Bible study groups with Pentecostal and Mennonite attendees. She also met with a Women's Institute. She joined in quilting and sewing activities.

Shortly after the Steinkes moved to Rock Creek, the Pentecostal church split into two groups. The Steinkes were very discouraged when no one attended a Vacation Bible School they had planned. On the third day, a Pentecostal member came to the Steinkes.

"Who is sponsoring this program?" she asked.

Eileen replied, "We are Seventh-day Adventists."

"I thought you were from the break-away Pentecostals. Had I known who you are I could have filled this room," she replied. With her help the attendance started and grew.

Melvin and Eileen decided to keep the VBS program going all winter. They invited their group to come to their home each Sabbath evening for Bible stories. Parents began to come with their children. As the group grew, the Steinkes opened their home for Sabbath services.

One interested family accepted an invitation to attend a seminar an hour away from Rock Creek. During the several days the seminar lasted, the two families became close friends. That Pentecostal family shared the news of the great seminar.

Well into the second year in Rock Creek the Steinkes had twenty persons attending services in their home. Many worshiped on both Sunday and Sabbath. Now, a Revelation seminar is planned. A Baptist family is preparing for baptism.

Melvin and Eileen are watching for the possibility of purchasing a church in the near future. They were delighted to discover a couple of former Adventists who are now renewing their commitment to the Lord Jesus.

The Steinkes are demonstrating Jesus' method of reaching out to people. Strong evangelism is built upon developing bonding friendships with others.

FROM ALCOHOLIC TO A GODLY MOTHER

Charlotte Walkus was an alcoholic. One day in 1978, while in the depths of despair, she uttered a very earnest prayer, "O Lord, please take me out of the gutter that I have put myself in."

The very next day a government worker serving the needs of her Native American nation in British Columbia, Canada, asked whether Charlotte would like to enroll in an alcohol treatment program. Charlotte replied, "Yes. Your coming today is an answer to my prayers."

Charlotte was surprised to learn that her friend Willie had also joined a program. The program lasted for six weeks. For five months Charlotte and Willie resisted the temptation to go back to drinking. In spite of their determination, however, they eventually returned to heavy drinking.

"I learned that I was trying to be sober in my own strength, and I failed miserably," Charlotte said. In 1980, at a very low point in her life, Charlotte gave her defeated life to the Lord. On November 27 she made a decision, "I don't care what anyone says, I am giving myself to Jesus."

"During my years as an alcoholic, I was a very poor mother," Charlotte testified. "Under the influence of drink, I often abused my children verbally and physically. Since Jesus has transformed my life, I have gathered all seven of my children and asked their forgiveness. Because Jesus has freed me from evil habits and has given me a new heart, Jesus has made me a better mother and example to my children."

In 1983 Willie and Charlotte were married. Charlotte praises God, "Our lives have been totally changed. We begin each day by giving ourselves to Jesus. We enjoy weekly fellowship with our brothers and sisters in our nation's church."

She continued with her testimony, "The biggest difference in our lives is having the Lord on our side and becoming godly parents to our children."

The transformed lives of Charlotte and Willie have become powerful examples for their children and friends to come to Jesus for help in daily living.

Charlotte says, "Since God has freed us from slavery to alcohol, we have a happy marriage. Our home has become a loving, peaceful place. Before, alcohol robbed us of all dignity and happiness."

Neighbors often call upon Willie and Charlotte to come to their homes and pray for them. They too want to be free from alcohol and drugs.

PRAYER TRANSFORMS A LIFE

Willie Walkus is a member of the Kwasala–makwaxda–xw nation located in Port Hardy in the northern tip of Vancouver Island in British Columbia, Canada. "I was an alcoholic for twenty years," Willie says. "I had no hope. I lived only to get another drink. I wandered the streets of Vancouver. Each night I hunted for shelter to sleep in. Often I slept on the city streets."

All during this time, Willie remembered his grandfather. Until his ninetieth birthday this godly ancestor prayed every day. "I knew that there was a God somewhere, but I kept on drinking."

The Kwasala–makwaxda–xw songs with which his grandfather filled his day kept running through Willie's mind in his few sober moments. Even in the darkest moments of his life Willie knew that somewhere the God of his grandfather was still there.

Willie had an aunt who was a follower of Jesus. On October 21, 1979, she concluded a week of fasting and prayer for Willie. As that week ended, Willie remembers a strange experience. "I reached for a drink. I held the bottle to my lips, but I could not swallow the alcohol."

Willie felt a strange sensation moving through his body. Then he became paralyzed. He could not speak. He felt that he was about to die. Someone called an ambulance, which rushed Willie to the hospital.

Lying helpless on a hospital bed, Willie prayed, "God, if You are there, please help me. I will serve You the rest of my life." God answered that prayer. But Willie returned to the streets. "I did not keep that promise. Soon I was drinking again."

Willie testifies that it is impossible for a sinner to keep promises in his own strength. Those promises always end in failure. In 1981 Willie prayed a different prayer, "Lord, I am Yours; please help me."

Willie began attending the forty-member church of his Kwasala–makwaxda–xw nation. A long period of spiritual growth began. When a young church member testified to the blessings of God when one tithes, Willie responded, "I don't earn enough to pay tithe." Little by little, Willie's understanding and experience grew. Today, he has experienced the windows of heaven being opened as God keeps His promise to faithful tithe payers.

"My life is exactly opposite to what I experienced during those twenty terrible years of alcoholism," he testifies. "My family has a new precious love from God. We have dear friends in our church."

Willie would like everyone to know, "No matter who you are or how far you have fallen into sin, God will hear your cry and come to help."

FAITHFUL HITCHHIKERS

When Clara Smith, a single parent living on the Navajo reservation in New Mexico, learned about a prophecy seminar that the All Nations Church in Gallup, New Mexico, was conducting, she decided to attend. She took her three teenage children with her. Night after night Clara and her children, Alexis, eighteen; Dana, seventeen; and LaCora, fourteen; made the eighty-mile round trip to attend the meetings. They were thrilled by the clear explanation of Bible truth that the pastor presented, and in November 1999 Clara and her children committed their lives to God in baptism.

Every Sabbath Clara and her teenagers faithfully made the trip in her aging auto to worship God with her new church family. Then, late one night as the family returned home after prayer meeting, a black cow wandered across the dark highway in front of her car. There was no time to stop, and Clara hit the cow.

No one was seriously injured, but the car was totaled. Clara had no insurance, and the cow's owner refused to repay her loss. Clara cannot work because she has rheumatoid arthritis; she had no money to replace the car. There are no other church members living anywhere near her to give her family a ride to church. But Clara and her family refused to let this setback keep them from their weekly appointments with God. Clara and her children prayed that God would help them get to church some other way.

Week after week, Clara and her children prayed for a ride, then set out to hitchhike to church. God has been faithful, and the family has not missed a single Sabbath. And they are never late, in spite of their irregular mode of transportation. They even attend prayer meeting, and once a month Clara and her children hitchhike to the church to take their turn cleaning it for Sabbath.

One Sabbath, a driver stopped to offer the family a ride. He asked where they were going. When Clara replied that they were going to church, the driver said, "I am on my way to work. When I reach my job, you may drive on to church. Just bring the car back to me when church is over."

The family continues to rely on God's providence and the kindness of strangers to get to church. But Clara and her children are determined not to miss Sabbath services. "I receive such a blessing as I worship with God's people," she said. "I cannot understand why some people don't attend church regularly."

THE ROBBERS REPENT

Every week Pastor Karro Rao gathered the tithes and offerings from the churches of his district in the South Western Mission of Papua New Guinea. He would then take them to the mission office. The weekly tithes and offerings usually amounted to nearly 3,000 *kinars* (US$1,500).

One week as he made his way along the narrow road, a bamboo pole suddenly fell across his pathway, and four robbers surrounded him. One wielded a knife; another a homemade gun. "Are you carrying money?" they asked.

"Yes," the pastor answered truthfully.

"Then hand it over," one man said.

"I can do that," the pastor answered. "But you must know that this money does not belong to me. I am a pastor. This money was given by my church members for the work of God. I have five *kinars* of my own money that I will give to you, but I urge you to not touch God's money."

"Give us all the money!" the robbers ordered threateningly.

Pastor Rao gave the bandits all the money he was carrying. After the bandits disappeared, Pastor Rao hurried to a telephone and called the mission office to report the theft. Then he asked the office staff to pray that God would help get the money back.

Six days later Pastor Rao was walking along the same pathway when a bamboo pole again dropped across the path in front of him. This time the pole had a plastic bag attached to it. It was his money bag. Before he could retrieve the bag, the same four criminals surrounded him. "Please take this money and give it for God's work," one man said.

Curious, the pastor asked, "What happened to make you change your mind?"

"We wanted to buy some beer and get drunk. But when we tried to open the bag of money, our hands began to shake so violently that we could not open it."

Pastor Rao answered, "Thank God! He loves you so much, and He has a better life planned for you. I am sure that you don't want to spend the rest of your life hurting people."

Pastor Rao developed a friendship with these men, and within a few months one of them was baptized. The others are still preparing to experience that better life that Pastor Rao promised them.

LANDING AT THE WRONG AIRSTRIP

Pastor Thomas Davai, president of the Western Highlands Mission in Papua New Guinea, boarded the mission plane to visit a remote congregation. Forty-five minutes later, the Cessna aircraft circled the tiny jungle strip. The entire village gathered to greet the plane.

But Pastor Davai did not recognize any church members. "Can you tell me whether there are any Christians here?" he asked the crowd.

"What is a Christian?" was the reply. "We have none of them in this place." Somehow, the pilot had landed on the wrong strip. This was the first visit of the mission plane to Tawa village.

Pastor Davai asked, "May we return sometime to visit you?"

"You are welcome to return anytime," the villagers replied.

Several months passed, then one day a man stopped by the mission office. He had been looking for the Christians who had come to his village. He remembered seeing the three-angel logo on the side of the mission airplane. And as he passed through the city streets he saw the same logo on a sign in front of the mission office. He had been looking for this three-angel sign.

As he stepped inside the office, he asked the receptionist if he could see the "big fella" of the church. He was ushered into Pastor Davai's office. How pleased he was to see the very man who had visited Tawa.

"We have been waiting for you to return to my village. Can you come and help my people?" was his request. Pastor Davai recognized a "call from Macedonia" in this village leader.

There is no access to Tawa by road. It takes a forty-minute flight to reach this distant village. Casenov, a lay missionary, was sent to survey Tawa and make plans to help the villagers.

The people of Tawa constructed a church and a pastor's home. Now there are several baptized members. Another forty persons have joined a "class ready" preparing for baptism. Pastor Davai is convinced that an angel guided the mission plane to land on the wrong airstrip, making it possible for Tawa to hear the gospel.

THE WAR OF THE BEES

Enemies were determined to destroy Laiagam, a village located in the eastern highlands of Papua New Guinea. For several weeks, warfare disturbed the entire community. Houses were burned to the ground. Several persons had been killed on both sides. Not only were spears and bows and arrows used, but a few villagers owned guns. The guns brought a new terror into the method of solving tribal differences.

To inflict as much hurt as possible, tribal warriors cut down trees, destroyed crops, and slaughtered animals. The war raged for almost one month.

A Christian church was located in Laiagam. Its situation was very dangerous. The two warring tribes were located on either side of Laiagam. During battles, weapons landed in Laiagam. Arrows with fire brands attached had destroyed several homes. The Christian church stood alone amidst the carnage.

The little group of believers decided the best course for them was to leave for a safer location. They made this decision in their beloved church. They felt that this would be the last time that they would see it standing.

However, one young member named Alo decided he would remain with the church. Shortly after the others left, he heard an advancing war party. They were headed for the church. He could see their lighted torches. In minutes the church would burn to the ground.

Alo fell to his knees. He earnestly prayed for help from God. "Lord help me do what I can to save this church." He picked up a piece of plastic pipe that had a funnel attached to one end. This homemade "trumpet" was used to call worshipers to the church. He gave the "trumpet" a loud blast and again asked God for help. The mob advanced to within a few meters of the church. Then a miracle happened. The sky seemed to darken.

A huge swarm of bees declared their own war against the attackers. Weapons were dropped. Now the mob was busy swatting bees and running wildly through the ruins of the village.

The church was saved. Alo's prayer made the difference. The congregation returned. What a precious praise meeting followed. "We know that God has saved our church. God sent His angels to direct the bees against our enemies."

WINNING SOULS IN THE MUD

He is youthful, handsome, and intelligent. With hard work Jason was certain of a great future. He was about to graduate from Moresby University in Papua New Guinea. His heart was filled with dreams of a good position, a good wage, and, one day, a family.

Then two occurrences completely changed his life. During his senior year, Jason attended an evangelistic meeting. As the Bible truths about Jesus and the gospel were presented, he accepted the message and gave his life to the Lord.

The second experience was less positive. With his bachelor's degree in engineering, Jason began a search for employment. But since only 30 percent of the population was employed, his search was not successful.

So at twenty-six years of age, he asked the Lord for direction. The answer came. Jason felt impressed to begin sharing his new faith. He further became convinced that he should go to the southern portion of Papua New Guinea that borders on the Gulf of Papua. This is a challenging, unentered area.

Mud and water cover this lowland province. Small villages are scattered on tiny islands surrounded by water and mud. Jason knew that the people who lived here faced many problems. There is a high rate of illiteracy. And the harsh environment causes stress. Most of the people had never heard the good news about Jesus.

With only a Bible in hand, and with his wallet empty, Jason made his way to the gulf area. He stopped at a village near Baimuru town and made an offer to the people, "If you will provide me with food and shelter, I will teach your people how to read. I will also need help with transportation costs from time to time." The villagers agreed.

The only possessions that Jason had were the clothing he wore and his precious Bible. This Book became his textbook. Villagers crowded about him to learn how to read. The light of the gospel dispelled the darkness of their spiritual emptiness as they learned to read the Word of God.

Bible study was followed by decisions to become Christians. A small group of believers was formed. Jason asked for transportation to the next island village. These villagers also accepted his offer to be their teacher.

When Pastor Keith Grolimund of the Papua New Guinea Union Mission stopped to visit Jason, he asked, "What things do you have for your work?"

The answer came back, "Sir, I have only this Bible."

Pastor Grolimund emptied his case of all the books he had. Now Jason was also able to teach his people gospel songs and enrich his teaching with other religious books. He is preparing 500 for baptism.

"PLEASE CALL ME NEWMAN"

When *The Quiet Hour* evangelistic program came to Mt. Hagen, Papua New Guinea, in 1991, a very curious man decided he would attend. However, he did not want any of his friends or neighbors to know that he was interested in religion.

He pulled his hat over his forehead and his sweater up over his nose. Only his eyes remained in view. Night after night he came in this disguise. He was impressed by the careful Bible documentation for what he heard. He purchased several books that were offered for sale following each evening meeting. The meetings came to a close. Six years passed. Then another *Quiet Hour* evangelistic team came to Mt. Hagen.

The well-dressed, highly educated man attended again. This time he made no effort to conceal his identity. On one of the last nights of the meetings he rose and told his story. He graphically portrayed his years of searching for God's truth. He told of attending the early *Quiet Hour* meetings while hiding his identity.

"I spent six years studying the Bible," he testified. "I know that I have now found a people who truly follow the Holy Bible. Next week I will be baptized. I am determined to follow Jesus for the rest of my life."

"Now I have a request to make," the man continued. "When I was christened I was given the name Damien. But I read in 2 Corinthians 5:17 that anyone in Christ is a new creation. Therefore, I will change my name. From the time of my baptism I want everyone to please call me by my new name, which will be Newman."

And truly Newman is a new man in Christ Jesus, as is every man who gives his life to Christ and His service.

THE CRIMINALS' CHURCH

Abel Ti's gang was well known in the community around Mt. Hagen, Papua New Guinea. They had terrorized the region so much that the community nearly became a ghost town. The gang's crimes filled villagers with fear.

Finally, the police caught Abel and put him in prison. He was expected to work six days a week with Sundays off. But, Abel noticed that some prisoners were excused from work assignments on Saturdays as well. They were Sabbath keepers. So Abel claimed to be a Sabbath keeper, too, in order to get Saturdays off work. He wanted to sleep all day Saturday, but was afraid that the guards might notice and make him work. So he decided to attend the Sabbath worship services.

Then Abel escaped from prison, and with two of his former gang members he hiked into the jungle. The trio built a bush house for themselves.

While they worked, Abel did some serious thinking. "We are not living right," he finally told his friends. "We need to change our ways. We should go to church. Let's go to the church in the village this week."

"No, we can't go there. We've hurt too many of those people. They will call the police, and we will be arrested again," his companions replied.

"Then we'll build our own church," was Abel's response.

The three men began gathering jungle material to build their own church. In a few days they had completed a little bush church beside their home. Now they began trying to conduct Sabbath services, with one man leading out while the other two sat on the bench. But they were very uncertain how to proceed.

One Sabbath a group of young people appeared. "Who are you?" Abel asked.

"We are Sabbath keepers," the youth replied. "We are attending school in town. We heard that there was a church up here, and we decided to visit."

"Would you please lead out in the services?" asked Abel.

The young people agreed, and now the three criminals sat and listened.

"Please come back every week. We want to know more about God."

The young people agreed, and the next weekend the criminals prepared for the return of the youth. But they failed to appear. When Abel learned that they had been confined to their dormitory rooms for leaving the previous week without permission, he took his rifle and headed for town. When he met the principal of the school Abel demanded that the youth be permitted to visit his church each week. The principal hastily agreed, and through the ministry of the youth the three criminals found Christ and a new life in Him.

84

"PLEASE COME, DADDY!"

The family stood by eight-year-old Kalinga's hospital bed. She awoke and whispered, "A man is coming to visit me." The family wondered who the man was. Later, when the Christian pastor entered Kalinga's room, she said excitedly, "He is the man that I saw in my dream!"

Kalinga's mother recognized the Christian pastor. She and her children had attended the church several times. She introduced the pastor to her husband, an officer in a large bank in Papua New Guinea. Father was always too busy to attend church. His every moment was filled with business contacts.

One Sabbath after Kalinga had returned home from the hospital, she saw her father loading his golf clubs into the car. He was on his way to play golf with some business friends. Kalinga asked him, "If Jesus were to come back today and ask me where you are, what should I tell Him? Do you want me to tell Him that you are playing golf?"

Kalinga's father was startled. He had never considered religion as important or thought of God as a person. He thought about his friends who were expecting him at the golf course.

Kalinga took her father's hand. "Daddy, today is Visitors' Day. I want you to be my visitor. Please, Daddy, come with me." The pleading look in his little daughter's eyes touched his heart. He put away his golf clubs and went to change into his suit.

Kalinga's mother was surprised when she saw her husband dressed up. "Where are you going this morning?" she asked.

"To church," he said. "It is Visitors' Day, and I am Kalinga's visitor."

That morning Kalinga did not go to her kindergarten class. "My daddy is a visitor. I will stay with him and help him make friends," she told her teacher.

Kalinga's father enjoyed church. When citywide evangelistic meetings were held in an outdoor field, he and his family attended—even on the nights when it rained. And when the meetings ended, Kalinga's father joined the baptismal classes.

Kalinga is so happy that God used her to help win her father to Jesus.

THE ROCK SPLIT IN TWO

Hidden among the 1,125 islands that make up the Marshall Islands is tiny Ebon Atoll, a circle of twenty-six islets in the Pacific. A huge rock juts out of the ocean near one of these islets. For years this rock has symbolized the Ebonites' resistance to change from outsiders. Ebonites say, "Many try to break Ebon, but it won't break." However, recent miracles have caused some to change their minds.

In 1996 Min Kong Wook from Korea and Alfred Barreta from the Philippines arrived on Ebon as young missionary volunteers serving with the 1,000 Missionary Movement. Neither knew Marshallese, the native language. The islanders were amazed when, after studying for only a few weeks, the two young men could read, sing, and speak Marshallese. "The Lord has done this for us," Alfred explained. The people called it a miracle.

Home for the two missionaries was a humble native hut. Their only light was a kerosene lamp. Food and water were often a problem. "When we ran out of food, we fished. If we caught fish, we ate. Sometimes we had only rice, unless we ran out before the supply ship arrived," Alfred said. The islanders catch rain for drinking and bathing. Despite these inconveniences, Alfred exclaimed, "God is so good!"

For years the islanders avoided Kejen, a cruel drunkard who bullied his neighbors. But Kejen was attracted to the missionaries, and soon he began studying the Bible with them. The islanders watched as the Holy Spirit transformed Kejen into a kind, gentle man who now looks for ways to help others. If a family is hungry, Kejen goes fishing and gives them his catch. His life became a powerful witness to the islanders of God's transforming power.

As the Ebonites saw evidence of God's power working in the lives of Alfred, Min, and Kejen, they began listening to the missionaries' message. Two Ebonite women were the first new believers baptized, after Kejen. On the night of their baptism, the rock that symbolized the Ebonites' resistance to change mysteriously split in two, as if cut by a large knife. Because the islanders believe God split the rock, they are now open to hearing the gospel.

At the time of this writing forty persons have been baptized. The believers meet in a tentlike structure that often blows down during storms and on windy days. The believers are planning for a simple church. "God has done some very special things for Ebon," say Min and Alfred.

A SPARK IGNITED

Warren Uziah lives in his wife's family village in North New Georgia, Solomon Islands. Warren recently became interested in his wife's Christian religion.

Warren decided to visit his father, who is chief in another village. Before he left, he asked his mother-in-law for some books and literature to take along to share in his village. She gave him some copies of *The Desire of Ages, Steps to Christ*, and *The Great Controversy*, as well as some magazines and tracts.

During his visit, Warren gave the books and tracts to people who seemed interested. And when he returned home, he gave his mother-in-law a list of people who wanted to take Bible studies by correspondence. She happily enrolled them in The Voice of Prophecy course.

One person who received a book from Warren was his cousin, Ron Kanga. As Ron began reading the book, he discovered several new ideas that caught his attention. The book gave him a clearer picture of God's plan for the universe and for his own life. By the time he finished reading the book, his life was changed.

Ron was so excited by what he had discovered that he began visiting people to share what he had learned. He started studying the Bible with several of his friends and relatives. Soon, he was studying regularly with twenty people in the village. Sometimes his studies lasted until long after midnight.

Ron wanted to be baptized, so he contacted the nearest mission and asked for someone to come and baptize him. A pastor came to visit him and question him about his knowledge of the Bible truth. Ron and his wife were baptized late in 1998.

Ron told the pastor that several of the people he was studying with in his village would soon be ready for baptism as well. The pastor asked Ron what he was using for Bible study materials. Ron answered simply, "Just these." And he held up his Bible and *The Great Controversy*. The pastor is confident that with Ron's zeal, his village will soon have a congregation worshiping God.

THE MECHANIC TURNED PREACHER

Beven Stephen lives on Guadalcanal, in the Solomon Islands. He grew up in a Christian home, but during his teens he drifted away from the church. He dropped out of school and took a job as an auto mechanic. He was a good one and quickly became the supervisor of the repair shop. He thought he had everything he wanted from life.

But a sudden and serious illness shattered his dreams. His doctor gave him little hope for recovery and suggested that Beven should prepare to die.

Beven's family and friends began praying for him, and God healed him. Beven returned to God and the church he had left as a youth. He began telling others what God had done for him. Soon he decided to quit his job as a mechanic and become a lay preacher, even though he had no training in preaching or evangelism.

He wanted to share his faith with people who knew nothing about Sabbath keepers. He chose Nagusa, a village in the remote mountains of Guadalcanal. He arrived in Nagusa and began sharing his faith. One local man told Beven to leave the village. When Beven did not leave, the man beat him. Beven still refused to leave.

The village chief, a convert from heathenism named Billy Graham, invited Beven to visit him. "I want to know two things," he told Beven. "What is the Bible basis for not eating pork and for worshiping on the Sabbath?"

Beven smiled and replied, "If you attend my meetings, I will explain these Bible teachings."

Chief Billy Graham agreed to attend the meetings and ordered the villagers to stop persecuting Beven. With this encouragement, Beven prepared for the public meetings. As a result of Beven's fervent prayers and faithful work, Chief Billy Graham and nine others took their stand for Christ and were baptized.

Beven is working to raise up a church in another village. But he has not forgotten the believers in Nagusa. He rejoices every time he learns of a baptism there. Today, fifty members worship together in Nagusa. The believers have begun construction of a church.

THE DOUGHNUT-SHAPED CLOUD

A group of youth went to an unentered area on an island near their homes to conduct meetings. After receiving permission from the leaders, the youth gathered jungle materials and built a shelter in which to hold public meetings.

It was hard work in the tropical sun. Heavy poles were set up to support the walls and roof. Smaller poles were tied in place for the frame of the building. Woven mats covered the walls, and a platform and benches were placed inside the building.

The youth invited villagers to the meetings that evening. The next morning the youth discovered that someone had torn down their building. Only a pile of materials remained.

With great effort the youth rebuilt their shelter in time for the evening meeting. But the next morning their hall was again in ruins. Again they rebuilt it. This happened again the next two days. On the fifth morning, the group found only ashes. There was no time to gather new materials and rebuild before their scheduled evening meeting.

They prayed for wisdom and help. An elderly gentleman approached. "I am sorry that my people have treated you this way. Come, I have materials at my home, and room for a building. I will help you." With praises to God, they built a new building.

The local religious leader who had ordered some ruffians to burn the building thought the youth would leave the village. He saw the new building and called the rough youth together. He gave each a bamboo torch. "Burn it to the ground," he ordered.

The Voice of Youth team heard of the plot; they rushed to the new hall and climbed onto the roof. As light from the torches encircled them, they pleaded for God's protection.

Then one by one the torches began to go out! It was raining all around them, but not on their little church. The rain fell from a doughnut-shaped cloud above the meeting hall!

News of the miracle spread through the village. Many were convinced of God's presence in the cloud and in the meetings the youth were conducting. Today this village has a church.

This is the spirit of Global Mission. As courageous members press into new areas, the Lord works with them and protects them.

CREATIVE EVANGELISM

I stood in the parking lot of the church in General Santos City in the South Philippines. The roar of motorcycle engines in the distance grew louder. As the motorcycles neared the church, they slowed down, then one by one they pulled into the church yard.

These motorcycles, equipped with a side car, served the city as taxis. Each taxi driver was a member of a Christian Taxi Association. The cyclists' leader excitedly told me that with their own funds they were conducting radio evangelism. One of their drivers was the "radio evangelist." Another was the announcer. Their program had been on the air for several months.

Now they were planning evangelistic meetings. All the expenses would come from their club budget. No wonder the General Santos church was overflowing with members! Satellite churches were planned in other parts of the city.

The children in the primary division also were holding evangelistic meetings. They had targeted twenty nonbelieving parents in the school most of the students attended. The children divided topics into three or four sections and memorized their sermonettes. Other children prepared special music, offered prayer, or announced during the program. Parents were invited to come to the meetings.

How touching it was to listen to a seven-year-old child tell the audience that Jesus is coming soon and to hear a child's voice read the Scriptures with power and understanding.

At the time of my visit the children had reached half of their goal—ten parents were being prepared for baptism by the pastor.

Members of the General Santos church have learned something every one of Christ's followers needs to know: Everyone's help is needed so that the commission to take the gospel to all the world can be completed. What are you doing to help?

LOVE WINS OVER HATE

"I hated the people of that tribe. For years the anger boiled in my heart." This is the testimony of Junnie Ree Pagunsan. It all started when tragedy struck a farming community on an island in the south Philippines. It was harvest time. When a ravaging enemy tribe attempted to take the crop, Junnie's uncle resisted. In the scuffle Junnie's uncle was killed, his aunt was raped, and the farm was taken.

This terrible experience happened when Junnie was a child. Upon the completion of his ministerial training, Junnie was invited to serve as a chaplain in a hospital that served the members of the hated tribe. Ninety percent of the patients were from that tribe. "It was hard for me to serve. I was constantly thinking of my uncle and aunt. I performed my duties with as little contact as possible."

Four years later, Junnie was invited to attend a seminar that discussed methods of cross-cultural evangelism. It was dealing with the culture and religion of the people that Junnie had hated for so long. The seminar group gathered each day to pray for the salvation of these people.

After the seminar, Junnie was offered a position on a team that was assigned to work for these people. During home visitation and small-group study, something happened in Junnie's heart.

"I began to see that these people were children of my heavenly Father. The Holy Spirit worked a miracle upon my heart." Daily, Junnie visited in homes and prayed with his new friends. He accepted invitations to eat with the tribal members and sleep in their homes. In his heart he now had a burden to help these people to know Jesus as Lord and Savior.

Junnie and his wife opened their home to the once-hated people. Precious fellowship developed as they ate at his table and spent the night in his home. At times Junnie and his wife hosted more than forty guests. During these visits Junnie shared the story of his love for Jesus.

It was a great thrill when the team that Junnie worked with began to construct a church for the converts. Junnie praises God that there are now more than 100 believers worshiping in the new chapel.

When asked, "Junnie, what are your plans for the future?" he replied, "I have dedicated my life to bringing as many of these people to the Lord as possible." Junnie now wears the clothing of the formerly hated tribe in an attempt to be one with them.

TAUGHT BY AN ANGEL

The people arrived at the beach in trucks, buses, jeeps, and motorcycles for the mass baptism following evangelistic crusades in the Philippines. After a worship service on the beach, thirty pastors stood in the crashing waves of the Pacific Ocean and baptized nearly 1,000 people. After the service, a man gave his testimony.

His name is Baget. He is a member of the B'Laan tribe, an animist people living on the island of Mindanao. For years he had robbed—and sometimes killed—his victims. He had earned a well-deserved reputation as a ruthless murderer and was feared by the community.

But one day a glorious being appeared to Baget. His face was kind and shone like the sun. He told Baget, "You must worship the God of heaven on Sabado (Sabbath), God's holy day." Then the being was gone. Baget was stunned. He tried to recall the being's words. Worship the God of heaven? On Sabado? This was something new to Baget. The Christians he had encountered all worshiped on Sunday. Why would this glorious being tell him to worship on another day?

The shining being returned to Baget several times. Each time he revealed more of what Baget must do to worship the true God. Baget told his village elders of the being's visits and messages. The villagers, impressed by the visions, decided to obey.

When missionaries entered the village who did not worship on Sabado, the villagers rejected their messages, for they did not teach the same truths as the glorious being. Then the local mission heard about the angel visits and sent a lay preacher to study with the people. As Baget and the villagers listened, they recognized that the lay preacher's teachings were the same as the glorious visitor's. They welcomed the lay preacher and joined his Bible studies.

Following evangelistic meetings, Baget brought twenty-five of his fellow B'Laan people to be baptized in the ocean in the mass baptism. Baget's life is a testimony to God's power to transform. Today, Baget teaches others about Christ. His old life is gone, and as a result of his testimony, nearly 200 new believers worship in the two churches Baget has helped to raise up.

JESÚS FINDS JESUS

While some people come to Christ in one giant step, others are guided by many faithful witnesses. The journey of Jesús Hagad of the Philippines started with one small voice.

"For seventeen years I served God as a priest," Jesús said. "Then one day a voice said to me, 'Jesus Christ is not in the Eucharist (the consecrated communion elements).' "

This revelation began a chain of questions in the priest's mind. *If Christ were not in the Eucharist, what other treasured church rituals were not based on God's Word?* As Jesús began to question his religious experience, he laid aside his prayer book and opened his heart to God in soul-searching prayer.

Feelings of guilt flooded over him as he realized that man-made rituals could not remove sin. He had no peace, because he was not sure that God forgave and accepted him. But, like Jacob, he continued to wrestle with God in prayer. He was thrilled to see God respond to his pleas. As he accepted Christ's promise of forgiveness, God became real to him. He found peace.

Jesús left the priesthood and joined a Protestant church. The Lord blessed him with a wife and four children, but he kept searching for more of God's truth. In early 1996 he attended evangelistic meetings where he learned that Sunday was not God's holy day. This revelation stunned him, but as he and his wife read the Bible texts upholding the Sabbath, they asked themselves how they could have kept Sunday for so many years when the Bible is so clear that the seventh day is the Sabbath of the Lord.

As Jesús learned more about Sabbath keeping, he remembered Sabbath-keeping children with whom he had attended school when he was a boy. He wanted his own children to live as those children had. He and his family prayed together, asking for God's forgiveness and direction. Jesús and his wife decided to follow God's leading to keep the Sabbath and were baptized along with their eldest daughter. Jesús testifies simply, "I did not find Jesus Christ in religious ceremonies, but I found Him in the Bible, and in His Sabbath."

THE POWER OF GOD'S WORD

The Philippines is a land of eighty-seven different tribal dialects. Bibles are available in the major languages, and Bible translators from the Wycliffe Bible Translators, at great personal sacrifice, spend years living in remote villages, learning the culture and language of a tribe, in order to produce at least a portion of God's Word in that language.

Pastor Albert Gulfan, president of the Central Philippine Union Conference, is a member of one of the minority tribes in the Philippines. His tribe numbers only about 300,000 and speaks a language called Masbateneo (mahs-bah-ten-AY-o).

Pastor Gulfan yearned to hold evangelistic meetings among his own people. Some of the villages had resisted previous attempts by various denominations to evangelize their areas. They threw a rain of stones on the roofs of the meeting halls and otherwise disrupted the meetings.

Pastor Gulfan arranged for teams of laymen to enter the area and lay the groundwork for the evangelistic series. Suspicious villagers watched their every move. They were impressed with the workers' friendliness and courtesy. When the workers announced a Vacation Bible School, mothers took their children, but stayed, ready to take their children home if they did not like what they heard. Soon, however, the mothers felt safe leaving their children to enjoy the meetings.

When Pastor Gulfan arrived for the meetings, he brought with him the first portion of the Bible printed in the Masbateneo language. The audience fell silent as they heard the words of God read in their own tongue—by a preacher from their own tribe! Resistance faded. Attendance at the meetings grew. At the close of the meetings, forty persons were ready for baptism. An additional fifty joined baptismal classes, including one man who is an official in the municipal government.

Pastor Gulfan praised God for the power of His Word and for the faithful translator who hopes to soon have the entire Bible translated into the Masbateneo language.

THE FAITHFUL CHIEF

As I stepped into the jungle clearing in the Philippines, I entered a primitive village called Dampaan. The entire village soon appeared to see the foreigner from America. The village chief, Tibulawan, welcomed me. During the visit, the chief made an appeal, "Please send us a teacher."

Several weeks later, two student missionaries from Mountain View College in the south Philippines arrived in Dampaan and started a school. The first-grade students ranged in age from six to twenty, all learning to read and write together. In the evenings, the villagers gathered to listen to student missionaries lead in Bible studies. Before that year was over Chief Tibulawan and twenty-six of his people were ready for baptism. Eventually, the entire village followed their chief's example and were baptized. Several weeks later, when I again visited Dampaan, I found a lovely little jungle chapel, which they had constructed from native materials, and the entire village worshiping God with the student missionaries.

The message of Christ's soon coming spread to other villages in the area. Then funds ran out, the overseas missionaries from Mountain View College left, and the student missionaries from the college no longer came to teach the people. Fifteen years passed. A new American missionary, Fred Webb, came to teach at Mountain View. He heard about the former school at Dampaan, and his curiosity was aroused. One Sabbath morning he decided to take a group of students and visit the site of the former mission school. No one knew they were coming. As they neared the village, they heard singing. To their joy they found the villagers worshiping God. Chief Tibulawan preached. Although unable to read, he quoted texts he had memorized. Brother Tibulawan had remained faithful during the long fifteen years they were without outside spiritual leadership, and he had held his village together in the worship of Jesus.

Mountain View College has again sent student missionaries to reopen the school at Dampaan and to renew the work among the Manobo people with schools in many villages.

During evangelistic meetings held in the Philippines in 1997, Chief Tibulawan brought more than twenty people down from the mountains to be baptized. The work is growing, and thousands of animist people from the mountains around Mountain View are now learning to know the Lord Jesus as their Savior.

If you enjoyed this book,
you'll enjoy these as well:

Mission Pilot

Eileen Lantry. The true adventures of David Gates, a missionary pilot who repeatedly experienced the miracles of God in his life. Through hijackings, prison, and many other narrow escapes, David proves that living for God is still the highest adventure.

0-8163-1870-0. Paperback.
US$12.99, Can$20.99.

Under the Shadow of the Rising Sun

Donald E. and Vesta West Mansell. For three years Don Mansell's world revolved between hunger, weevils, lack of privacy, and numbing routine as a prisoner of the Japanese army in the Philippines. Through the eyes of a survivor, we see the intervention of Providence in an unforgettable true-life WWII adventure.

0-8163-1976-6. Paperback.
US$14.99, Can$23.99.

Though Bombs May Fall

Penny Young Sook Kim, Richard A. Schaefer, and *Charles Mills.* The extraordinary story of George Henry Rue, an Adventist missionary doctor who left a lucrative medical practice in the U.S. to serve the Korean people during the war years. This is the story of many determined individuals who wrenched success from tragedy.

0-8163-1963-4. Paperback.
US$10.99, Can$17.99.

Order from your ABC by calling **1-800-765-6955**, or get online and shop our virtual store at <www.AdventistBookCenter.com>.

- •Read a chapter from your favorite book.
- •Order online.
- •Sign up for email notices on new products.